CHECK YOUR ENGLISH
VOCABULARY FOR

IELTS

Rawdon Wyatt

A & C Black • London

www.acblack.com

First edition published 2001
by Peter Collin Publishing

Reprinted 2002, 2005

A & C Black Publishers Ltd
37 Soho Square, London W1D 3QZ

© Peter Collin Publishing 2001
© A & C Black Publishers Ltd 2005

A CIP entry for this book is available from the British Library

ISBN 0 7136 7604 3

A & C Black uses paper produced with elemental chlorine-free pulp,
harvested from managed sustainable forests.

Text typeset by A & C Black
Printed in Italy by Legoprint

About this workbook

Introduction

This workbook has been written for students who are planning to sit either the general training or the academic modules of the IELTS exam. It covers some of the main vocabulary points that you will need for, or come across in, the listening, reading, writing and speaking sections of the exam.

We hope that you find the modules in this book useful and that the vocabulary you acquire will help you to achieve the grade you want in the IELTS.

Good luck!

Structure of the IELTS Workbook

Each vocabulary area is presented in the form of a self-contained module with task-based activities which present each vocabulary item in a real context.

- Pages 1-53 focus on general vocabulary items which can be used in all aspects of your English. Some of these are relevant to specific tasks in the IELTS exam (for example, describing how something works, writing a letter or describing a table).

- Pages 54-101 focus on topic-specific vocabulary areas which may be required in the exam (for example, education, business and industry or global problems). Each module consists of three tasks: the first two present vocabulary items in context, and the third gives you the opportunity to review the vocabulary in the form of a gap-fill exercise.

Using the IELTS Workbook

You should not go through the modules mechanically. It is better to choose areas that you are unfamiliar with, or areas that you feel are of specific interest or importance to yourself.

Recording Vocabulary

Remember that you should keep a record of new words and expressions that you acquire, and review these on a regular basis so that they become a part of your active vocabulary.

Extending Your Vocabulary

Also remember that there are other methods of acquiring new vocabulary. For example, you should read as much as possible from a different variety of authentic reading materials (books, newspapers, magazines, etc).

Using an English Dictionary

To help you learn English, you should use an English dictionary that can clearly define words, provide information about grammar and give sample sentences to show how words are used in context. You can use any good learner's English dictionary with this workbook, but it has been written using the material in the *Easier English Dictionary for Students* (ISBN 0 7475 6624 0), published by Bloomsbury Publishing (www.bloomsbury.com/reference).

International English Language Testing System (IELTS)

This workbook has been written to help you improve your vocabulary when working towards the *International English Language Testing System* (IELTS) examination. The IELTS English examination is administered by the University of Cambridge Local Examinations Syndicate, The British Council and IDP Education Australia. For futher information, visit the *www.ucles.org.uk* website.

Contents

PAGE	TITLE
General Vocabulary	
1	Condition
2	Changes 1
4	Describing & analysing tables
6	How something works
7	Writing a letter
8	Presenting an argument
9	Contrast & comparison
10	Location
12	Joining/becoming part of something bigger
13	Reason & result
14	Generalisations & specifics
16	Focusing attention
17	Opinion, attitude & belief
18	Stopping something
19	Time
20	Objects & actions
22	Likes & dislikes
24	Obligation & option
25	Success & failure
26	Ownership, giving, lending & borrowing
27	Groups
28	Around the world
30	Size, quantity & dimension
32	Shape & features
33	Emphasis & misunderstanding
34	Changes 2
36	Opposites
38	Addition, equation & conclusion
39	Task commands
40	Confusing words & false friends
44	Useful interview expressions
45	Phrasal verbs 1
46	Phrasal verbs 2
48	Phrasal verbs 3
49	Phrasal verbs 4
50	Phrasal verbs 5
52	Spelling
Topic-Specific Vocabulary	
54	Education
56	The media
58	Work
61	Money & finance
63	Politics
65	The environment

PAGE	TITLE
67	Healthcare
69	Travel
71	Crime & the law
73	Social tensions
75	Science & technology
78	Food & diet
80	Children & the family
82	On the road
84	The arts
87	Town & country
89	Architecture
92	Men & women
95	Geography
97	Business & industry
100	Global problems
Answers	
102	Answers
123	Vocabulary record sheets

For reference, see the *Easier English Dictionary for Students* (0 7475 6624 0)

Condition

A. Look at these sentences. They all use 'if'. Rewrite each sentence, replacing 'if' with the words in *bold*. You may need to remove some of the other words.

1. You can borrow my dictionary if you return it before you go home.
   providing that

2. You can't go to university if you don't have good grades.
   unless

3. Pollution will get worse if we continue to live in a throwaway society.
   as long as

4. Many developed countries are willing to waive the Third World debt if the money is reinvested in education and medicine.

   on condition that

5. Some countries will never be able to rectify their deficits even if they work very hard.
   no matter how

6. Computers are difficult things to understand, even if you read a lot of books about them.
   however many

7. Crime is a problem, even if you go to relatively safe countries.
   wherever

B. Now rewrite each sentence beginning with the words in *bold*. For example:

Providing that you return it before you go home, you can borrow my dictionary.

C. Complete these sentences using an appropriate word or expression from above and your own ideas.

1. British universities will accept students from abroad _____

2. Working for a large company can be a fulfilling experience _____

3. Most banks are happy to lend customers money _____

4. The government will reduce income tax _____

5. The environmental situation will continue to worsen _____

6. There will always be long waiting lists at our hospitals _____

7. Travelling helps you understand more about the world around you _____

D. Some nouns can be used to express condition. Complete these sentences 1-3 with one of the words from A, B or C.

1. Being able to drive is one of the _____ of the job of salesman.
   A. prerequirements   *B. prerequisites*   *C. prescriptions*

2. Before you accept a job, it is important that you agree with the _____ of the contract.
   A. conditionals   *B. conditions*   *C. conditioners*

3. It is a _____ of the university that you attend an interview.
   A. requirement   *B. requisite*   *C. requiem*

1

Changes 1

Look at the pairs of sentences in 1-20 and choose a verb from the box which can be used with both sentences. In some cases, the meaning of the verb may change slightly. Then use a dictionary to find other objects which can be used with the verbs.

adapt • adjust • alter • cure • demote • disappear • dissolve exchange • expand • fade • increase • promote • reduce • renew renovate • replace • swell • switch • transform • vary	

1. We need to_____ these cars so disabled people can drive them.

   The country found it hard to _____ to the new government

2. To make sure your car is safe, you should check and _____ the brakes on a regular basis.

   He found it hard to _____ to living in a tropical country.

3. You must _____ the voltage or the system will blow up.

   He decided to _____ his appearance by having plastic surgery.

4. Our bills will be less if we _____ from gas to electricity.

   They had to _____ flights at Heathrow Airport.

5. You can't _____ the terms of the contract once it has been signed.

   He wants to _____ his appearance.

6. It will help your digestion if you _____ your diet.

   Prices of flats _____ from a few thousand to millions of pounds.

7. We need to _____ our pounds for dollars.

   You can usually _____ goods which are faulty if you show the receipt.

8. We have had to _____ our sales force to cope with the extra demand.

   Water will _____ when it is frozen.

9. The price of oil will _____ next year.

   Most bosses refuse to _____ salaries when they are asked.

2

10. The management decided to _____ the
company and sell the offices.

_____ the sugar in boiling water.

11. More and more people are moving to cities to
_____ the population there.

The wasp sting caused his leg to _____ up.

12. The market for typewriters will
probably_____ completely in the next
few years.

The police are baffled by the increasing number
of people who _____ each year.

13. The old contract ran out and we had to
_____ it.

Many people argue that it's futile to _____
old hostilities.

14. They have received funds to _____ the
old buildings.

The house is in good structural condition, but we
need to _____ the central heating system.

15. The boss offered to _____ him from
salesman to manager.

Our main aim is to _____ tourism in
the country.

16. They wanted to _____ me from
manager to salesperson.

If we _____ you, you will lose a large
part of your salary.

17. If you wash it too much, the colour will
_____ .

We watched the islands _____ away
into the distance.

18. The company decided to _____ the
permanent staff with freelancers.

You must _____ the books on the shelf
when you have finished with them.

19. The doctors were unable to _____
her illness.

_____ the meat in salt water for
between three and five days.

20. Governments are trying to _____
pollution.

The best way to save money is to _____
the number of staff.

For reference, see the *Easier English Dictionary for Students* (0 7475 6624 0)

Describing & analysing tables

A. Look at the four tables below. These show demographic trends in four different countries between 1996 and 2000. The numbers on the left and right of each table show the number of people in hundred thousands. Using the information in these tables, match sentences 1-13 on the next page with the appropriate country. Use the words and expressions in *bold* to help you.

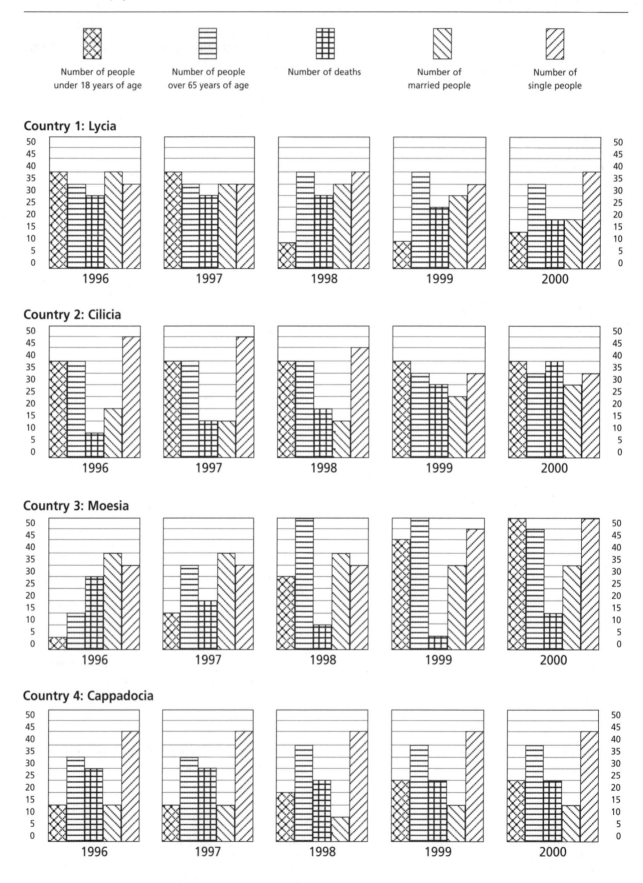

Number of people under 18 years of age

Number of people over 65 years of age

Number of deaths

Number of married people

Number of single people

Country 1: Lycia

Country 2: Cilicia

Country 3: Moesia

Country 4: Cappadocia

For reference, see the *Easier English Dictionary for Students* (0 7475 6624 0)

Describing & analysing tables

1. In which two countries was there a **considerable discrepancy** between married and single people between 1996 and 1998?

2. In which country was there a **constant** and **considerable discrepancy** between married and single people over the five-year period?

3. In which country was there a **sudden** and **noticeable difference** between those under 18 and those over 65 in 1998?

4. In which country did the number of under-18s **rise dramatically** between 1996 and 2000?

5. In which country did the number of under-18s **increase slightly** between 1996 and 2000?

6. In which country did the number of over-65s **go up sharply** between 1996 and 1998?

7. In which country did the number of married people **decline significantly** over the five-year period?

8. In which country did the number of deaths **decrease significantly** between 1996 and 1999?

9. In which two countries was there a **slight decline** in the number of married people between 1998 and 1999?

10. In which country was there a **sharp drop** in the number of under-18s between 1997 and 1998?

11. In which country was there a **slight reduction** in the number of deaths over the five-year period?

12. In which country was there a **significant increase** in the number of deaths between 1998 and 2000?

13. In which country did the number of deaths **remain constant** over the five-year period?

B. Now look at the table below, which shows the changes in economic activity in a town over a period of five years. The figures on the left and right show the number of people involved in these activities, in thousands. Write your own sentences to describe the situation in the town regarding the number of:

1. People employed in industry between 1996 and 2000.

2. People employed in retail between 1996 and 2000.

3. People employed in public services between 1999 and 2000.

4. People employed in tourism between 1996 and 2000.

5. Unemployed between 1998 and 2000.

6. People employed in industry compared with those in retail in 1996.

7. People employed in industry between 1998 and 1999.

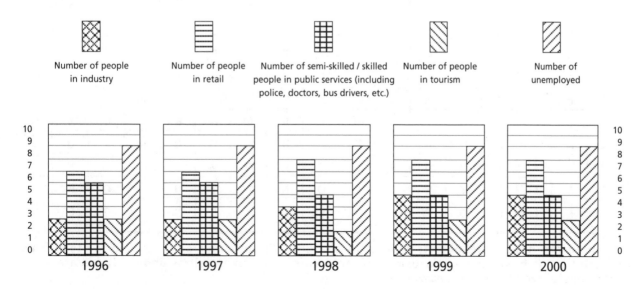

Number of people in industry

Number of people in retail

Number of semi-skilled / skilled people in public services (including police, doctors, bus drivers, etc.)

Number of people in tourism

Number of unemployed

1996   1997   1998   1999   2000

For reference, see the *Easier English Dictionary for Students* (0 7475 6624 0)

How something works

A. Look at these sentences and decide which object is being described in each one. Use the words in *bold* to help you. You will find the objects hidden in the word grid at the bottom of the page.

1. The most important part of this object is a strip of two different metals, one on top of the other. As they *heat up*, both metals *expand,* but one does it faster than the other. The strip *bends* and *connects* with a switch, which *turns off* the power supply. When the strip *cools down*, the metals *contract* and the switch is *disconnected*. (1 word)

2. This object has several *component parts*, most of which are made of plastic. A disc inserted into the object *spins* quickly. At the same time a thin beam of light *strikes* the disc and *converts* digital symbols into sounds. These sounds can be *increased* or *decreased* in volume by means of a button or dial. (3 words)

3. Liquid and gas are *compressed* in a hard metal tube. This can be *released* by *pushing* or *squeezing* a button which *opens* a valve. When the liquid-gas combination *leaves* the tube and is mixed with oxygen, it rapidly *expands*. (1 word)

4. This object is mainly *made of* aluminium. As it *moves* forward, air *flows* over two horizontal sections. As it *accelerates*, a vacuum is *formed* over the horizontal sections and the object is pulled into the air by the force of this vacuum. (1 word)

5. This object consists of two main parts; one is made mainly of plastic and metal, the other is made mainly of glass. Light *enters* the glass section and a small door in the device *opens* up when a button is *pressed*. At the same time, a smaller window called an aperture *adjusts* itself to control the amount of light. The light is then *absorbed* by a sheet of plastic coated in a special chemical. An image is *formed* and this can then be *processed* and *developed* into a two-dimensional paper-based object. (1 word)

6. A sharp blade inside a plastic container *rotates* very quickly. It *chops* or *grinds* anything it touches, which we can then use to *produce* soup, sauces and dressing. (2 words)

7. This is a very simple object which originated in China. A small piece of paper is *lit* with a match. It *burns* away until the flame *ignites* the chemical compound inside a cardboard tube. The result is a display of light and colour. (1 word)

Q	C	A	R	E	N	G	I	N	E	W	E	R	T	T	Y	U
A	S	D	F	G	H	J	K	L	Z	X	C	V	B	O	N	M
B	A	L	L	P	O	I	N	T	P	E	N	A	Q	A	C	W
Q	W	E	R	F	O	O	D	P	R	O	C	E	S	S	O	R
B	T	Y	U	I	O	P	A	D	S	A	G	R	K	T	M	J
I	A	M	N	B	K	E	T	T	L	E	V	O	C	E	P	T
C	E	C	X	Z	L	K	J	H	G	F	D	S	S	R	U	H
Y	R	S	A	P	O	I	U	Y	T	R	E	O	E	W	T	E
C	O	M	P	A	C	T	D	I	S	C	P	L	A	Y	E	R
L	P	L	K	J	H	G	F	D	S	A	Q	W	E	R	R	M
E	L	I	G	H	T	B	U	L	B	M	N	B	V	C	X	O
C	A	M	E	R	A	I	F	I	R	E	W	O	R	K	U	S
L	N	K	J	H	G	F	D	S	A	Q	W	E	R	T	Y	T
T	E	L	E	V	I	S	I	O	N	T	Y	U	I	O	P	A
M	I	C	R	O	W	A	V	E	O	V	E	N	N	G	E	T

B. There are nine more objects hidden in the grid. Choose *four* of them and write a brief description of how they work, using the bold words and expressions above. There are some more useful words in the answer key (on page 103).

For reference, see the *Easier English Dictionary for Students* (0 7475 6624 0)

Writing a letter

A. Below, you will see eleven common situations that people encounter when they are writing a formal letter. Choose the sentence or phrase (A, B or C) that would be most appropriate in each situation.

1. You are writing a letter to the headteacher of a school or college, but you don't know their name. How do you begin your letter?
    A. Dear headteacher   *B. Dear Sir / Madam*   *C. Dear Sir*

2. You have received a letter from the manager of a company which buys computer components from your company, and you are now replying. What do you say?
    A. Thank you for your letter.   *B. Thanks a lot for your letter.*   *C. It was great to hear from you.*

3. You recently stayed in a hotel and were very unhappy with the service you received. You are now writing to the manager. What do you say?
    A. I had a horrible time at your hotel recently.   *B. I would like to say that I am unhappy about your hotel.*   *C. I would like to complain about the service I received at your hotel recently.*

4. You have sent a letter of application to a college, together with your curriculum vitae which the college requested. What do you say in the letter to explain that your curriculum vitae is attached?
    A. You asked for my curriculum vitae, so here it is.   *B. As you can see, I've enclosed my curriculum vitae.*   *C. As you requested, I enclose my curriculum vitae.*

5. You have applied for a job, but you would like the company to send you more information. What do you say?
    A. I would be grateful if you would send me more information.   *B. I want you to send me more information.*   *C. Send me some more information, if you don't mind.*

6. In a letter you have written to a company, you tell them that you expect them to reply. What do you say?
    A. Write back to me soon, please.   *B. Please drop me a line soon.*
    C. I look forward to hearing from you soon.

7. In a letter you have written, you want the recipient to do something and are thanking them in advance of their action. What do you say?
    A. Thank you for your attention in this matter..   *B. Thanks for doing something about it.*
    C. I am gratified that you will take appropriate action.

8. The company you work for has received an order from another company and you are writing to them to acknowledge the order and let them know when you can deliver. What do you say?
    A. About the order you sent on 12 January for....   *B. I would like to remind you of the order you sent on 12 January for...*   *C. I refer to your order of 12 January*

9. In a letter, you explain that the recipient can contact you if they want more information. What do you say?
    A. Give me a call if you want some more information.   *B. If you would like any more information, please do not hesitate to contact me.*   *C. If you would like any more information, why not get in touch?*

10. You began a letter with the recipient's name (e.g., Dear Mr. Perrin). How do you end the letter?
    A. Yours faithfully   *B. Yours sincerely*   *C. Best wishes*

11. You did not begin the letter with the recipient's name (see number 1 above). How do you end the letter?
    A. Yours faithfully   *B. Yours sincerely*   *C. Best wishes*

B. Look at these sentences and decide if they are true or false.

1. Formal letters are always longer than informal letters.

2. In a formal letter it is acceptable to use colloquial English, slang and idioms.

3. In a formal letter it is acceptable to use contractions (e.g., *I've* instead of *I have*)

4. In a formal letter you should include your name and address at the top of the page.

5. In a formal letter, you should always write the date in full (e.g., 1 April 2000 and not 1/4/00).

6. In a formal letter, you should always put your full name (e.g., James Harcourt and not J. Harcourt) after your signature at the bottom of the letter.

7. Formal letters do not need to be broken into paragraphs. It is acceptable to write them as one continuous paragraph.

For reference, see the *Easier English Dictionary for Students* (0 7475 6624 0)

Presenting an argument

A. Read the text below, in which somebody is trying to decide whether to go straight to university from school, or spend a year travelling around the world. Put their argument into the correct order, using the key words and expressions in *italics* to help you. The first one and last one have been done for you.

A (1)   I'm really in two minds about what to do when I leave school. Should I go straight to university or should I spend a year travelling around the world?

B.   *It is often said that* knowledge is the key to power, and I cannot disagree with this.

C.   *On the one hand,* I would experience lots of different cultures.

D.   Unfortunately, *another point is that* if I spent a year travelling I would need a lot of money.

E.   And I'm not alone in this opinion. *Many consider* a sound career and a good salary to be an important goal.

F.   *However,* it could be argued that I would also meet lots of interesting people while I was travelling.

G.   *Secondly,* if I go straight to university, I'll learn so many things that will help me in my future life.

H.   *First of all,* there are so many benefits of going straight to university.

I.   But *I believe that* it would be easy to make a bit while I was travelling, giving English lessons or working in hotels and shops.

J.   *Moreover,* I'll be able to take part in the social activities that the university offers, and meet lots of new friends who share the same interests.

K.   *The most important point is that* the sooner I get my qualifications, the quicker I'll get a job and start earning.

L.   *Nevertheless,* these inconveniences would be an inevitable part of travelling and would be greatly outweighed by the other advantages.

M.   *In my opinion,* starting work and making money is one of the most important things in life.

N.   *On the other hand,* I could end up suffering from culture shock, homesickness and some strange tropical diseases.

O.   *Furthermore,* if I spent a year travelling, I would learn more about the world.

P. (16)   All right, I've made my mind up. Now, where's my nearest travel agency?

B. Using the key words and expressions in italic from the last exercise, present an argument for *one* of the following issues:

1.   A government's main priority is to provide education for its people.

2.   The only way to save the environment is for governments to impose strict quotas on the energy we use (for example, by restricting car ownership, limiting the water we use).

3.   Satisfaction in your job is more important than the money you earn.

4.   Living in a town or city is better than living in the countryside.

5.   It is our responsibility to help or look after those less fortunate than ourselves (for example, the homeless, the mentally ill).

For reference, see the *Easier English Dictionary for Students* (0 7475 6624 0)

Contrast & comparison

Complete these sentences with the most appropriate word or expression from A, B or C.

1. The two machines _____ considerably. One has an electric motor, the other runs on oil.

    A. differ   B. differentiate   C. differential

2. The _____ in weather between the north and the south of the country is very noticeable.

    A. comparison   B. contrast   C. compare

3. Many people cannot _____ between lemon juice and lime juice.

    A. differ   B. differentiate   C. contrast

4. Children must be taught to _____ between right and wrong.

    A. differ   B. contrast   C. distinguish

5. There is a _____ between being interested in politics and joining a political party.

    A. distinguish   B. distinctive   C. distinction

6. Can you tell the _____ between a good boss and a bad one?

    A. difference   B. differentiate   C. contrast

7. The management must not _____ between male and female applicants.

    A. differ   B. contrast   C. discriminate

8. Asia covers a huge area. _____ , Europe is very small.

    A. By way of contrast   B. By ways of comparing   C. By similar means

9. The new model of car is very _____ to the old one.

    A. same   B. similar   C. common

10. Her political opinions are _____ to mine.

    A. same   B. exactly   C. identical

11. Some political parties have such similar manifestoes that they are difficult to _____ .

    A. tell apart   B. say apart   C. speak apart

12. My friends and I enjoy doing many of the same things. In that respect, we have a lot _____ .

    A. in similar   B. in particular   C. in common

13. There seems to be a large _____ between the number of people employed in service industries, and those employed in the primary sector.

    A. discriminate   B. discretion   C. discrepancy

14. British and Australian people share the same language, but in other respects they are as different as _____ .

    A. cats and dogs   B. chalk and cheese   C. salt and pepper

15. Britain's economy is largely based on its industry, _____ a few hundred years ago it was an agrarian country.

    A. while   B. whereas   C. whereby

9

Location

A. Look at this diagram and complete the sentences opposite using the expressions listed below. In some cases, more than one answer is possible.

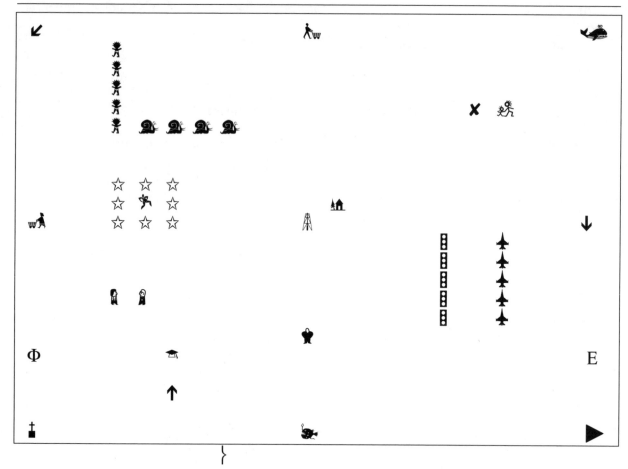

...directly opposite...	...stands outside...
...on the right-hand side of...	...halfway between...
...in close proximity to...	...in the bottom left-hand corner of...
...to the left of...	...at right angles to/perpendicular to...
...to the right of...	...roughly in the middle of...
...at the bottom of...	...on the left-hand side of...
...in the bottom right-hand corner of...	...parallel to...
...surrounded by...	...at the top of...
...in the top left-hand corner of...	...in the top right-hand corner of...
...exactly in the middle of...	

For reference, see the *Easier English Dictionary for Students* (0 7475 6624 0)

Location

1. The ↓ is _____ the ✈

2. The ⚚ is _____ the ☆

3. The ⚲ is _____ the diagram

4. The ⚑ is _____ the diagram

5. The Φ is _____ the E

6. The ♟ is _____ the ⚒ and the ⚓

7. The ⚒ is _____ the diagram

8. The ⛪ is _____ the diagram

9. The ⚐ is _____ the diagram

10. The ↙ is _____ the diagram

11. The ⚑ is _____ the ⚑

12. The ⚑⚑⚑ are _____ the ⚑⚑⚑

13. The ✗ is _____ the ⚔

14. The 🐋 is _____ the diagram

15. The ⚓ is _____ the diagram

16. The ⚲ is _____ the ↑

17. The ↓ is _____ the diagram

18. The ▶ is _____ the diagram

19. The ⚭ _____ the diagram

B. How well do you know your country? Write the name of a city, town, village or island which...

1. _____ is situated in the middle of your country.

2. _____ is built on the slopes of a mountain.

3. _____ is located on the coast.

4. _____ stands on a cape or peninsula.

5. _____ is built on the edge of a river or lake.

6. _____ is a two-hour journey by car or bus from the capital.

7. _____ is a short distance off the coast.

8. _____ is about 10 miles (approximately 16 kilometres) from your home town.

Don't forget to keep a record of the words and expressions that you have learnt, review your notes from time to time and try to use new vocabulary items whenever possible.

For reference, see the *Easier English Dictionary for Students* (0 7475 6624 0)

Joining/becoming part of something bigger

The sentences below all contain a word or expression in *italics* which is related to the idea of two or more things joining together, sometimes with the result that they become part of something bigger. However, the words and expressions have all been put into the wrong sentence. Put them into their correct sentence. In some cases, more than one answer is possible.

A. Move the verbs into the right sentences.

1. His salary is *merged* to the cost of living, and increases on an annual basis.

2. The International Book Association *blended* with Universal Press in 1999 to form the International Press.

3. To get a better finish, he *swallowed up* the two paints together.

4. The firm *integrated* with its main competitor in the battle to win more customers.

5. The suggestions from all the committees were *took over* into the main proposal.

6. The immigrants faced hostility when they were first *incorporated* into the community.

7. A lot of students had problems before they *amalgamated* into college life.

8. When the large international college *got together* the smaller school, a lot of people lost their jobs.

9. The students *linked* one evening and decided to protest about their situation.

10. A large international company *assimilated* our firm last month and started making immediate changes.

B. Move the nouns into the right sentences.

1. The *alloy* between England and France came close to breaking down many times during the nineteenth century.

2. The *synthesis* between England and Scotland is over 300 years old.

3. In 2003, the three regional organizations responsible for helping homeless people formed a national *blend* to help and support one another.

4. Brass is a well-known *alliance* of copper and zinc.

5. Water is a *coalition* of hydrogen and oxygen.

6. The plan is a *unification* of several earlier proposals.

7. The *merger* of Italy did not occur until the second half of the nineteenth century.

8. The company made its fortune by selling a popular *union* of coffee.

9. The proposed *federation* of the Liberal and Labour Parties in the election was cause for much ridicule.

10. As a result of the *compound* with the other company, Flax International became the largest in its field.

For reference, see the *Easier English Dictionary for Students* (0 7475 6624 0)

Reason & result

A. Join the first part of a sentence in the left-hand column with a second part from the right-hand column, using an appropriate expression showing reason or result from the central column. In some cases, more than one of the expressions from the middle is possible.

1. The police asked him his...	...ensued...	...pass his exams
2. He failed his exam...	...effects of...	...wake anyone
3. A persistent cough...	...prompted him to...	...was unable to enroll for the course.
4.. She started haranguing the crowd...	...on account of...	...upsetting me like that?
5. He spent the whole weekend revising...	...as a consequence...	...his lack of revision
6. They came in quietly...	...affect...	...starting a riot
7. He refused to lend anyone money...	...owing to...	...its low turnover and poor sales history
8. The bank manager refused to lend the company more money...	...on the grounds that...	...its action
9. The school was forced to close...	...so as not to...	...when the police officers on trial were acquitted.
10. What were your...	...with the aim of...	...a large earthquake?
11. What are the...	...in order to...	...people rarely repay a loan
12. Stress and overwork can...	...consequences of...	...seek professional medical help
13. The army attacked without considering the...	...motives in...	...different people in different ways
14. He failed to send off his application form and...	...due to...	...poor student attendance
15. Riots and street fighting...	...reason for...	...speeding through the town

B. Now complete these sentences with an appropriate expression from the central column of the table above.

1. Panic buying _____ when the stock market crashed.

2. People often do things without considering the _____ their actions.

3. The government raised the income tax rate _____ curb inflation.

4. The government raised the income tax rate _____ curbing inflation.

5. The government raised the income tax rate _____ the rapidly rising rate of inflation.

6. When questioned, many racists cannot give a logical _____ their attitudes towards other racial groups.

7. The soaring crime rate alarmed the police superintendent and _____ adopt a zero-tolerance policing policy.

8. He was arrested _____ he was a danger to others and himself.

9. The family was forced to economise _____ go heavily into debt.

10. The fumes from motor traffic _____ people in many different ways.

For reference, see the *Easier English Dictionary for Students* (0 7475 6624 0)

Generalisations & specifics

A. Match the sentences in the list below with an appropriate sentence in the list opposite. The _underlined expressions_ in the first list should have a similar meaning to the words or expressions in _bold_ in the second list.

FIRST LIST

1. **_Small items of information_** are very important in a curriculum vitae.

2. I need to have **_precise information_** about your new proposals.

3. The plan was unable to go ahead because of a **_small important detail which is important in order to make something happen._**

4. He demanded to know the **_small, precise and sometimes unimportant details._**

5. When you read a piece of text in the exam, you should read it quickly first to get the **_general idea._**

6. Before you write an essay, you should plan it first and give a broad **_description without giving much detail._**

7. **_Odd features or details which make something different_** make the world a more interesting place.

8. Saying that all seventeen-year-olds take drugs is a bit of a **_general statement._**

9. Many cars have very similar **_typical features._**

10. The huge rise in computer sales is a good **_example_** of the direction in which technology is heading.

11. **_Normally,_** most students sitting the exam manage to pass with a good grade.

12. The new library **_shows a good example of_** British architecture at its best.

13. Before you travel somewhere, it is important to **_make a detailed list of_** things that you need to take.

14. French fries with mayonnaise is a dish which is **_an odd feature or detail of_** Belgian cuisine.

15. The article **_shows as an example_** his views on the way the company should develop.

Don't forget to keep a record of the words and expressions that you have learnt, review your notes from time to time and try to use new vocabulary items whenever possible.

For reference, see the *Easier English Dictionary for Students* (0 7475 6624 0)

Generalisations & specifics

SECOND LIST

A. Please let me have **the specifics** as soon as possible.

B. It's very frustrating when a minor **technicality** puts a stop to your plans.

C. In the same way, kimchii is a concoction of cabbage, chilli and garlic which is **peculiar to** Korea.

D. You should include full **details** of your past experience.

E. Once you have an **outline,** you will discover that your work is easier to organise.

F. We must be careful not to make this kind of **generalisation.**

G. **Itemise** everything in order of importance, beginning with your passport and visa.

H. As far as he was concerned, the **minutiae** could not be overlooked.

I. Most manufacturers are aware that these **characteristics** are what help sell their product.

J. It also provides us with an accurate **illustration** of the advances we have made in the last twenty years.

K. It **illustrates** his preference for increased automation.

L. Once you have the **gist,** it should be easier to understand it.

M. It **exemplifies** the style that is becoming increasingly popular with town planners.

N. In **general,** the average result is a B or C.

O. For example, it one of the **peculiarities** of the British system that judges and lawyers wear wigs in court.

B. Write a list of the words and expressions in bold above. Put them into two groups based on whether they are talking about general things or specific things. Try to give examples of each word in a sentence of your own.

> *Don't forget to keep a record of the words and expressions that you have learnt, review your notes from time to time and try to use new vocabulary items whenever possible.*

For reference, see the *Easier English Dictionary for Students* (0 7475 6624 0)

Focusing attention

A. Rearrange the letters in *bold* to form words which are used to focus attention on something. They all end with the letters -LY. Write the words in the grid underneath. If you do it correctly, you will find another word used to focus attention in the bold vertical box.

1. They reduced pollution *pislmy* by banning cars from the city centre during the rush hour.

2. The strange weather at the moment is *gaerlly* due to the El Niño phenomenon.

3. We're examining *iilmprary* the financial aspects of the case.

4. People *ilnamy* go on holiday in the summer.

5. The library is *veceslxuily* for the use of students and staff.

6. It's a *ilaptarrculy* difficult problem which we hope to resolve as soon as possible.

7. The advertisement is *elcifipcsaly* aimed at people over 50.

8. Some western countries, *otbanly* Canada and the United States, have a very high standard of living.

9. The staff are *stomly* women of about twenty.

10. Our trip to Poland was *rpeluy* an educational visit.

11. My home town is famous *hfiecly* for its large number of schools and colleges.

The word in the in the bold vertical box fits into this sentence:

The company trades _____ in the Far East.

B. Divide the words above into two groups, one group being the words which mean _only_ or _solely_, and one group being the words which mean _in most cases_ , _normally_ or _the main reason for something_.

Only or solely	In most cases, normally or the main reason for something

For reference, see the *Easier English Dictionary for Students* (0 7475 6624 0)

Opinion, attitude & belief

A. The words in *italics* in the following sentences are all used to talk about opinion and belief. However, the words are <u>grammatically incorrect</u> (for example, a noun has been used instead of an adjective, or a verb has been used instead of a noun, etc.), or sometimes a noun has been used which has the wrong meaning. Put the words into their correct form.

1. In my *opinionated*, technology is moving too quickly.

2. As far as I am *concerning,* happiness is more important than money.

3. Scientists are *convincingly* that human degradation of the environment is causing thousands of species to become extinct.

4. The government are *regardless* the Third World debt as a major barrier to global economic development.

5. Hundreds of people called the television station to register their *disapprove* of the presenter's behaviour.

6. She *maintenance* that most young people would rather work than go to school.

7. Do you *reckoning* that there will be an election in the next two years?

8. We strongly *suspicion* that the proposal to develop the computer facilities will not go ahead.

9. I *doubtful* that the new government will keep all its promises.

10. Do you *disapproval* of smoking?

11. I take strong *except* to people coming late or cancelling appointments at short notice.

12. A lot of people are *fanatic* about sport in general and football in particular.

13. British health inspectors are *obsession* about cleanliness in restaurant kitchens.

14. After years of struggle, the *moderations* have gained control of the party.

15. He has very *conservatism* views and disapproves of change.

16. The government are *commitment* to the struggle to end institutional racism in the police force.

17. She was *dedication* to her family and would do anything to protect them.

18. They come from a strongly *tradition* family who still believe in arranged marriages.

B. Put these nouns and adjectives, which describe people's beliefs, under the most appropriate heading in the table. Can you think of any other words or expressions that you could add?

| opinionated • a republican • pragmatic • a Muslim • an intellectual |
| a revolutionary • tolerant • a moralist • narrow-minded • bigoted |
| open-minded • a vegan • left-wing • right-wing • a socialist • a royalist |
| a Buddhist • a conservative • a liberal • a communist • a vegetarian • dogmatic |
| moral • a fascist • religious • a Hindu • middle-of-the-road • an anarchist • a stoic |

Political beliefs	Personal convictions and philosophies

For reference, see the *Easier English Dictionary for Students* (0 7475 6624 0)

Stopping something

For each of the examples 1-15, choose an appropriate verb from the box which best fits the description and can be used in the sample sentence.

> back out • sever • quash • suppress • deter • dissuade • give up • cancel
> remove • turn down • put an end to • delete • repeal • rescind • deny

1. To cut out part of a document, a computer file, etc.
   To stop your hard disk becoming too full, you should _____ *any unwanted programmes.*

2. To officially end a law so that it is no longer valid.
   The new government Bill seeks to _____ *the existing legislation.*

3. To discourage someone from doing something.
   The threat of severe punishment didn't _____ *the thieves from striking again.*

4. To persuade someone not to do something.
   The college tries to _____ *students from entering exams which are not suitable for them.*

5. To annul or cancel a contract or agreement.
   The committee decided to _____ *its earlier resolution on the use of its premises.*

6. To limit or suddenly stop something, such as a person's freedom.
   The military government attempted to _____ *the democracy movement by arresting its leaders.*

7. To end something suddenly and finally.
   The Cornucopian government decided to _____ *relations with Utopia.*

8. To refuse something which is offered.
   You should never _____ *a good job when it's offered to you.*

9. To decide not to support or be part of a project or activity after you have agreed to do so.
   We decided to _____ *when we discovered the company was in financial difficulty.*

10. To state that something is not correct.
    Before his trial, his lawyer advised him to _____ *embezzling company funds.*

11. To stop something which has been planned.
    There is no refund if you _____ *your holiday less than three weeks before the date of the departure.*

12. To make a judging or ruling no longer valid.
    He applied for a judicial review to _____ *the verdict.*

13. To stop doing something that you have done for quite a long time.
    You should _____ *smoking if you want to feel healthier.*

14. To stop something which has been going on for a long time.
    They agreed to _____ *their long-standing dispute.*

15. To take something away.
    I would be grateful if you would _____ *my name from your mailing list.*

For reference, see the *Easier English Dictionary for Students* (0 7475 6624 0)

A. Use the time clauses in the boxes to complete the sentences. Pay particular attention to the words that come before or after the time clause.

Part 1: One action or situation occurring before another action or situation

prior to • previously • earlier • formerly • precede • by the time

1. _____ the advent of the Industrial Revolution, pollution was virtually unheard of.

2. _____ the army had restored order, the city had been almost completely devastated.

3. _____ known as Burma, the republic of Myanmar is undergoing a slow and painful political transformation.

4. A sudden drop in temperature will usually _____ a blizzard.

5. It was my first trip on an aeroplane. _____ I'd always gone by train.

6. The Prime Minister made a speech praising charity organisations working in Mozambique. _____ that day he had promised massive economic aid to stricken areas.

Part 2: One action or situation occurring at the same time as another action or situation

while/as/just as • during/throughout • at that very moment • in the meantime/meanwhile

1. _____ the minister was making his speech, thousands of demonstrators took to the streets.

2. _____ the speech they jeered and shouted slogans.

3. The minister continued speaking. _____ the police were ordered onto the streets.

4. He finished the speech with a word of praise for the police. _____ people began throwing bottles and bricks, and the riot began.

Part 3: One action or situation occurring after another action or situation

afterwards • as soon as / once / the minute that • following

1. _____ the earthquake, emergency organisations around the world swung into action.

2. _____ the stock market collapsed, there was panic buying on an unprecedented scale.

3. The Klondike gold rush lasted from 1896 to 1910. _____ the area became practically deserted overnight.

B. Look at these words and expressions and decide if we usually use them to talk about (1) the past, (2) the past leading to the present, (3) the present or (4) the future. Try to write a sentence for each one.

for the next few weeks • as things stand • ever since • in medieval times
nowadays • from now on • back in the 1990s • over the past six weeks
over the coming weeks and months • in another five years' time • one day
in those days • a few decades ago • lately • at this moment in time
at the turn of the century • in my childhood / youth • at this point in history
by the end of this year • for the foreseeable future • for the past few months
last century • these days • from 1996 to 1998 • sooner or later

19

For reference, see the *Easier English Dictionary for Students* (0 7475 6624 0)

Objects & actions

A. The words in the box describe the actions of the things in 1-37. Match each action with the thing it describes.

evaporate • explode • change • melt • fade • bounce
crumble • trickle • rise • sink • ring • contract • crack • escape
stretch • wobble • congeal • burn • spill • smoulder • erupt • spin
revolve • set • flow • slide • rotate • spread • erode • meander
turn • subside • freeze • grow • expand • vibrate • float

1. The planet Earth moving round on its axis. _____

2. A washing machine in its final stage of a wash. _____

3. The moon moving around the Earth. _____

4. The CD-ROM tray on a computer base unit. _____

5. A house slowly sinking into soft ground. _____

6. Water slowly being converted into vapour. _____

7. Cooking fat becoming solid on an unwashed plate. _____

8. Traffic moving smoothly along a motorway. _____

9. Water changing from a liquid to a solid because of the cold. _____

10. Glass changing from a solid to a liquid in very high heat. _____

11. A loose wheel on a car. _____

12. Gas coming out of a faulty valve. _____

13. A rubber ball hitting the ground and going back into the air. _____

14. Loose windows in a window frame when a large vehicle passes nearby. _____

15. The population of a town becoming bigger. _____

16. A T-shirt which has been washed so often it has lost its colour. _____

17. The sun coming up in the morning. _____

18. The sun going down in the evening. _____

19. A wheel on a slow-moving train. _____

20. Traffic lights going from red to amber to green. _____

21. Cliffs being slowly destroyed by the sea. _____

22. Documents being laid out on a table. _____

For reference, see the *Easier English Dictionary for Students* (0 7475 6624 0)

23. A wide river winding through the countryside. _____

24. The sun turning people on a beach bright red. _____

25. An incense stick in the entrance to a temple. _____

26. A lump of dry earth being rubbed between somebody's fingers. _____

27. Cold metal as it gets hotter. _____

28. Hot metal as it gets cooler. _____

29. A piece of elastic being pulled so that it becomes longer. _____

30. A window being hit by a stone so that a long, thin break is formed. _____

31. Coffee falling out of a cup by mistake. _____

32. A bomb suddenly blowing up. _____

33. An alarm clock suddenly going off. _____

34. A boat going to the bottom of a river. _____

35. Dead fish lying on the surface of a polluted lake. _____

36. A volcano throwing out lava and ash. _____

37. Orders for a new product arriving at a company very slowly. _____

B. Several of the words in the box on the previous page can have more than one meaning. Use your dictionary to check which ones, then complete these sentences below with an appropriate word. You will need to change the form of most of the words.

---

1. The queues for the embassy were so long they _____ all the way down the street.

2. "What do you think you're doing?" he _____ angrily.

3. The government decided that the best economic course would be to let the dollar _____ .

4. Prices have been _____ steadily all year.

5. The light from the torch began to _____ as the batteries ran out.

6. The twig _____ loudly as he stood on it.

7. After the rainstorms passed, the floodwaters gradually _____ .

8. The discussion _____ around the problem of student accommodation.

9. The doctor _____ his broken arm.

10. The car _____ out of control on the icy road.

For reference, see the *Easier English Dictionary for Students* (0 7475 6624 0)

Likes & dislikes

A. Look at the words and expressions in the box and decide if they have a positive connotation (for example, they tell us that somebody *likes* something) or a negative connotation (for example, they tell us that somebody *dislikes* something).

loathe	yearn for	passionate about	fond of	captivated by
fancy	keen on	look forward to	dread	long for
appeal to	detest	cannot stand	repel	attracted to
fascinated by	tempted by	disgust	revolt	cannot bear

B. Now look at these pairs of sentences. Sometimes, both sentences are correct, sometimes one of them is wrong (for example, the construction is wrong) or it does not sound natural. Decide which ones.

1. A. It was well-known that he was loathed by the other teachers.

   B. It was well-known that the other teachers loathed him.

2. A. Sometimes I yearn for some time on my own.

   B. Sometimes some time on my own is yearned for.

3. A. Sport is passionate about by a lot of people

   B. A lot of people are passionate about sport.

4. A. Animals are quite fond of by British people.

   B. British people are quite fond of animals.

5. A. The first time I visited Venice, I was captivated by the city.

   B. The first time I visited Venice, the city captivated me.

6. A. Going to the cinema tonight is fancied by me.

   B. I fancy going to the cinema tonight.

7. A. From a young age, the idea of travelling was keen on me.

   B. From a young age I was keen on the idea of travelling.

8. A. I look forward to hearing from you soon.

   B. To hearing from you soon I look forward.

9. A. It is a well-known fact that students dread exams.

   B. It is a well-known fact that exams are dreaded by students.

For reference, see the *Easier English Dictionary for Students* (0 7475 6624 0)

10. A. Most children long for the long summer holiday to arrive.

    B. The long summer holiday is longed for by most children.

11. A. His sense of humour is appealed to by watching other people suffer.

    B. Watching other people suffer appeals to his sense of humour.

12. A. Racism is really detested by me.

    B. I really detest racism.

13. A. A lot of people cannot stand the long British winters.

    B. The long British winters cannot be stood by a lot of people.

14. A. The idea of living in a cold country repels me.

    B. I am repelled by the idea of living in a cold country.

15. A. She was attracted to the tall, handsome man who had helped her.

    B. The tall, handsome man who had helped her attracted her.

16. A. I have always been fascinated by information technology.

    B. Information technology has always fascinated me.

17. A. Were you tempted by his offer of a job in Australia?

    B. Did his offer of a job in Australia tempt you?

18. A. His mannerisms and habits disgusted me.

    B. I was disgusted by his mannerisms and habits.

19. A. Bigoted, arrogant people revolt me.

    B. I am revolted by bigoted, arrogant people.

20. A. Getting up early in the morning cannot be born by me.

    B. One thing I cannot bear is getting up early in the morning.

> *Don't forget to keep a record of the words and expressions that you have learnt, review your notes from time to time and try to use new vocabulary items whenever possible.*

For reference, see the *Easier English Dictionary for Students* (0 7475 6624 0)

Obligation & option

A. Look at sentences 1-10 and decide if the explanation which follows each one is true or false. Use the words and expressions in *bold* to help you decide.

1. During the exam, a pencil and eraser are *required*.
    The people organising the exam will provide you with a pencil and an eraser.

2. Parents can be made *liable for* their children's debts.
    Parents may be legally responsible for the money their children owe.

3. He was *obliged to* pay back the money that he had won.
    He had the choice whether or not to pay back the money that he had won.

4. Students doing holiday jobs are *exempt from* paying income tax.
    Students doing holiday jobs pay a smaller amount of income tax than other people.

5. The United Nations voted to impose *mandatory* sanctions on the country.
    The United Nations imposed legally-binding sanctions which had to be obeyed by everyone, without exception.

6. The doctors *forced* him to stop smoking.
    The doctors asked him to stop smoking.

7. It was an emergency and she pressed the red button; there was *no alternative.*
    There was nothing else she could do; she had to set off the alarm by pressing the red button.

8. Classes on Wednesday afternoons are *optional.*
    It is necessary to attend classes on Wednesday afternoons.

9. It is *compulsory* to wear a crash helmet on a motorcycle.
    It is your choice whether or not to wear a crash helmet when you ride a motorcycle.

10. The museum is asking visitors for a *voluntary* donation of £2.
    You don't need to pay £2 to visit the museum.

B. Complete these sentences with an appropriate word or expression from the exercise above. In some cases, more than one answer may be possible.

1. Visitors to the country are _____ to declare any excess tobacco or alcohol imports to the customs officer.

2. I'm afraid I have _____ but to resign from the committee.

3. If you are caught speeding, you will be _____ the payment of the fine.

4. Attendance at all classes is _____ , otherwise you may not get a certificate at the end of the course.

5. Many retired people do _____ work in their local community.

6. In some countries, there is a _____ death sentence for all drug traffickers.

7. For visitors to Britain from outside the European Union, a visa may be _____ .

8. He said he was innocent, but the police _____ him to confess.

9. Most new cars come with _____ air-conditioning.

10. Children's clothes are _____ from VAT.

> *Don't forget to keep a record of the words and expressions that you have learnt, review your notes from time to time and try to use new vocabulary items whenever possible.*

For reference, see the *Easier English Dictionary for Students* (0 7475 6624 0)

Success & failure

A. Match the first part of each sentence in the left-hand column with its second part in the right-hand column using an appropriate word from the central column. These words should collocate with the _underlined_ words in the right-hand column. In most cases, it is possible to use the words in the central column with more than one sentence.

SUCCESS

1. The two warring countries managed to...	...secure...	...his **ambitions** of being promoted to marketing manager.
2. During his first year as President he managed to...	...accomplish...	...my **aims** of doing well at school and then going to university.
3. The company couldn't afford to move to new premises but were able to...		...an **agreement** for a new lease.
4. He worked hard at his job and was soon able to...	...attain...	...its **targets** - those of free education and healthcare - within eight years.
5. The country badly needed to increase its overall standard of living and attempted to...	...achieve...	...his **obligations** to his current employer.
6. After four years of hard work, the motor racing team managed to...	...fulfil...	...their **goal** of becoming millionaires.
7. He desperately wanted to start a new job, but first of all he had to...		...their **dreams** of winning the Monaco Grand Prix.
8. Many people want to be rich but few...	...realise...	...a **lot more** than his predecessor had in the previous five.
9. I have a lot of plans, and one of them is to...	...reach...	...a **compromise** over the terms for peace.

B. Complete these sentences with an appropriate word or expression from A, B or C.

FAILURE

1. The People's Foundation Party decided to _____ its plans to establish a coalition government with the Democratic Liberal Party.

   A. abate   **B. abandon**   **C. abhor**

2. Peace talks between the two countries _____ , with neither side able to agree on terms.

   A. collapsed   **B. collaborated**   **C. collared**

3. Progress in the talks _____ when the inevitable impasse was reached.

   A. faulted   **B. faltered**   **C. fondled**

4. Our planned visit to the Czech Republic _____ because we were unable to get the visas.

   A. fell over   **B. fell down**   **C. fell through**

5. The company _____ with debts of over £1 million.

   A. faulted   **B. folded**   **C. foiled**

6. Their plans to impose stricter import quotas _____ when the European Bank declared their actions illegal.

   A. mistook   **B. mislead**   **C. misfired**

For reference, see the *Easier English Dictionary for Students* (0 7475 6624 0)

Ownership, giving, lending & borrowing

A. Complete sentences 1-13 with an appropriate word from the box. In some cases, more than one answer may be possible.

NOUNS

> donation • possessions • lease • owners • tenants • rent • property
> mortgage • estate • proprietors • belongings • landlords • loan

1. The law ensures that _____ respect the privacy of the people who live in their houses.

2. _____ of restaurants across the country protested at the new government tax that was put on food.

3. Private car _____ were hit the hardest when tax on petrol was increased.

4. The price of commercial _____ has almost doubled in the last four years.

5. When the recession hit, he was forced to sell his 250-acre _____ .

6. Many families lost all their _____ when the river flooded.

7. Put your _____ in the locker and give the key to the receptionist.

8. We will need to relinquish the offices when the _____ runs out at the end of the year.

9. They applied to the World Bank for a _____ to help pay off their balance of payments deficit.

10. A lot of people lost their homes when the interest rate rose so much they were unable to pay off their _____ .

11. The _____ complained to the council that the house they were living in was overrun with vermin.

12. The law does little to protect families who are thrown out of their homes because they are unable to pay the _____ .

13. Everybody is being asked to make a _____ to help the victims of the disaster.

B. The words in *bold* have been put into the wrong sentences. Decide which sentences they should belong in. In some cases, more than one answer is possible.

VERBS

1. Banks will refuse to *rent* money to anyone without sufficient collateral.

2. If you want to *contribute* a room in the centre of the city, you should be prepared to pay a lot of money.

3. The best way to see the country is to *provide* a car from an agency for a couple of weeks.

4. Companies *allocate* from banks to finance their business.

5. It is not only the wealthy who *provide for* money to charities.

6. It is our responsibility to *leave* our parents when they get old.

7. The government will tax you heavily for any money that your relatives may *lend* for you in their will.

8. Local councils will *borrow* free accommodation to the most needy on a first-come, first-served basis.

9. Charities such as the Red Crescent *hire* free medical aid to areas hit by disasters.

For reference, see the *Easier English Dictionary for Students* (0 7475 6624 0)

Groups

A. Put these words into the table based on the group of things they usually refer to.

| batch • huddle • heap / pile • company • stack • team • litter |
| swarm • flock • platoon • bundle • herd • throng • gang • crowd |
| bunch • set • pack • staff • group • crew • cast • shoal / school |

People in general	People working together	Animals	Objects

B. Complete these sentences using one of the words from the above task. In some cases, more than one answer is possible.

1. After the election, the huge _____ danced in the street.
2. The refugees sat in a small, tight _____ underneath some trees.
3. The first prize was a _____ of cheap saucepans.
4   The school is closed because the _____ are on strike.
5. The theatre _____ benefited from a government grant.
6. Following an outbreak of BSE, a _____ of cows has been destroyed.
7. The company processed a _____of orders.
8. A _____ of football fans wandered around the street breaking shop windows.
9. Half the _____ of the film were nominated for Oscars.
10. They threw the weapons in a _____ on the ground.
11. A small _____ of people petitioned the Prime Minister outside his house.
12. The _____ of fish that had been caught were deemed inedible owing to pollution in the water.
13. We were all surprised when our dog gave birth to a _____ of puppies.
14. Cabin _____ on aircraft are drilled in safety procedure.
15. As winter approaches, the _____ of geese fly south to warmer climes.
16. Half the football _____ were sent off in disgrace.
17. The stars had difficulty making their way through the _____ of people outside the cinema.
18. A _____ of soldiers from the Third Infantry have been charged with human rights abuses.
19. The immigrant arrived clutching nothing but a _____ of personal possessions.
20. A _____ of flowers is always an acceptable gift if you visit someone.
21. We were unable to open the door because a _____ of boxes was blocking it.
22. The women fell on the surprised burglar like a _____ of wild dogs.
23. The harvest was destroyed by a huge _____ of insects.

C. The following words all refer to groups of people meeting for a specific purpose. Match the words with their definitions below.

| delegation • tribunal • symposium • seminar • lecture • tutorial |

A. students listening to a talk on a particular subject
B. a group of representatives (for example, of a union) who want to explain something to someone
C. a student or small group of students who attend a teaching session
D. a meeting organised to discuss a specialised subject
E. a small group of university students discussing a subject with a teacher
F. a specialist court outside the main judicial system which examines special problems and makes judgements

For reference, see the *Easier English Dictionary for Students* (0 7475 6624 0)

Around the world

A. Choose the correct geopolitical word in A, B or C to complete each of these sentences.

1. Japan, Korea and the Philippines are all in the _____ .
    A. Near East   **B. Middle East**   **C. Far East**

2. The South Pole is situated in the _____ .
    A. Arctic   **B. Antarctic**   **C. Antarctica**

3. New Zealand is part of _____ .
    A. Australia   **B. Australasia**   **C. Austria**

4. Bangladesh is part of _____ .
    A. the Indian subcontinent   **B. India**   **C. Indiana**

5. Nicaragua is a country in _____ .
    A. North America   **B. South America**   **C. Central America**

6. Argentina, Brazil, Colombia, Panama and Honduras all form part of _____ .
    A. Latin America   **B. Spanish America**   **C. South America**

7. Apartheid was abolished in _____ in the 1990s.
    A. southern Africa   **B. North Africa**   **C. South Africa**

8. The United Kingdom and the Republic of Ireland form a group of islands known as _____ .
    A. Great Britain   **B. England**   **C. the British Isles.**

9. The United Kingdom and the Republic of Ireland form part of _____ .
    A. Continental Europe   **B. Mainland Europe**   **C. Europe**

10. Kuwait, Oman and the United Arab Emirates form part of what is known as_____ .
    A. the West Indies   **B. the Gulf States**   **C. the European Union**

11. Norway, Sweden, Finland and Denmark are known collectively as _____ .
    A. the Baltic Republics   **B. the Caribbean**   **C. Scandinavia**

> *Don't forget to keep a record of the words and expressions that you have learnt, review your notes from time to time and try to use new vocabulary items whenever possible.*

For reference, see the *Easier English Dictionary for Students* (0 7475 6624 0)

B. Change each country / area below into the nationality and / or language spoken of the people who come from that place (for example: Britain = British). Write each word in the appropriate space in the table. Be careful, because usually we add or remove letters to / from the name of the country before we add the ending.

Greece •	Portugal •	Ireland •	Belgium •	Finland •	England
Wales •	Scotland •	Holland •	Lebanon •	Malaysia •	Norway
Sweden •	Thailand •	Peru •	Bangladesh •	Israel •	Japan
Iran •	Burma •	America •	Canada •	Spain •	Turkey
Switzerland •	Saudi Arabia •	Denmark •	Iraq •	Australia •	Malta
Kuwait •	Russia •	Yemen •	Philippines •	Poland	

-ese (e.g., China = Chinese)	-(i)an (e.g., Brazil = Brazilian)	-ish (e.g., Britain = British)	-i (e.g., Pakistan = Pakistani)	-ic (e.g., Iceland = Icelandic)	Others (e.g., France = French)

C. A quick quiz. Answer these questions.

1. What do we call a variety of language spoken in a particular area? Is it an *accent*, a *dialect* or an *idiom*?

2. What is *your* mother tongue?

3. What do we call a person who is able to speak (a) two languages and (b) three or more languages fluently?

4. With regard to your country, what is (a) the name of the continent in which it is located, (b) the main language spoken and (c) the nationality of the people?

For reference, see the *Easier English Dictionary for Students* (0 7475 6624 0)

Size, quantity & dimension

A. Look at the following list and decide whether we are talking about something *big* (in terms of size, quantity or dimension) or something *small*.

1. a *minute* amount of dust _____

2. a *minuscule* piece of cloth_____

3. an *enormous* book _____

4. a *mammoth* job _____

5. a *huge* waste of time _____

6. a *vast* room _____

7. a *gigantic* wave _____

8. a *tiny* car _____

9. a *monumental* error _____

10. a *colossal* statue_____

11. *plenty* of food _____

12. *dozens* of times _____

13. a *narrow* alleyway_____

14. a *giant* building _____

15. a *gargantuan* meal _____

16. a *wide* avenue _____

17. a *broad* river _____

18. a *tall* man_____

19. a *high* mountain _____

20. a *deep* lake _____

21. a *shallow* pool _____

22. a *long-distance* journey _____

23. a *vast* crowd of supporters_____

24. *tons* of work _____

25. a *great deal of* time _____

B. Now complete these sentences using one of the expressions above. In some cases, more than one answer is possible.

1. Before you embark on _____ , it is essential that you are well-prepared.

2. We spent _____ working on the plans for the new library.

3. I've told you _____ not to smoke in here.

4. _____ must have blown into the camera and scratched the film.

5. Villages along the coast were destroyed when _____ caused by the earthquake swept houses into the sea.

6. It was _____ going there; he didn't even turn up.

7. One of the Roman emperor Nero's greatest excesses was to build _____ of himself in the city centre.

For reference, see the *Easier English Dictionary for Students* (0 7475 6624 0)

Size, quantity & dimension

8. Despite the poor harvest, there was _____ for the whole population.

9. _____ called the Thames separates the city of London from the suburbs to the south.

10. _____ gathered to see their favourite football team.

11. We ate _____ and then lay down to rest.

12. It was _____ and his voice echoed around the walls.

13. We have _____ to do in the next few days, so I suggest we start as soon as possible.

14. Loch Ness is _____ in the Highlands of Scotland.

15. The only evidence was _____ which was stuck on a branch of one of the trees in the garden.

16. 'Sumo' is _____ containing almost 1,000 pictures by the controversial photographer Helmut Newton.

17. He had _____ to do, so took the phone off the hook, made himself some coffee and sat down at his desk.

18. The Matterhorn, _____ in Switzerland, has claimed the lives of many who have tried to climb it.

19. He made _____ in his calculations and had to start all over again.

20. The manufacturers have built _____ which is ideal for getting around the city.

21. The NEC in Birmingham is _____ which is used for concerts and exhibitions.

22. The main feature of the town is a _____ lined with shops and cafés.

23. I could see the key glittering at the bottom of _____ .

24. Legend spoke of _____ dressed in gold, known as El Dorado.

25. _____ ran along the side of the house to a garden at the rear.

For reference, see the *Easier English Dictionary for Students* (0 7475 6624 0)

Shape & features

A. (Shape) Match the words below with the picture that best represents each word.

1. pyramid	2. cube	3. crescent	4. spiral	5. cone	6. sphere
7. rectangle	8. triangle	9. square	10. circle	11. cylinder	12. oval

A   B    C   D    E   F

G    H   I   J   K   L

B. (Shape) Look at the following list of words and decide what the correct adjective form is, A, B or C.

1. sphere	_____	**A. spherous**	**B. spherical**	**C. spherocous**
2. cube	_____	**A. cubed**	**B. cubous**	**C. cubal**
3. cone	_____	**A. conacular**	**B. conous**	**C. conical**
4. rectangle	_____	**A. rectanglous**	**B. rectanglis**	**C. rectangular**
5. triangle	_____	**A. triangular**	**B. trianglous**	**C. triangled**
6. circle	_____	**A. circled**	**B. circulous**	**C. circular**
7. square	_____	**A. square**	**B. squaret**	**C. squarous**
8. cylinder	_____	**A. cylindrous**	**B. cylindal**	**C. cylindrical**

C. (Features) Match the descriptions on the left with the objects, geographical features, etc., on the right.

1. a sharp edge with jagged teeth	_____	A. a country road in very poor condition
2. steep, with a pointed peak	_____	B. somebody's hair
3. rolling, with undulating wheat fields	_____	C. a very old tree
4. curved, with a smooth surface	_____	D. a knife
5. flat, with words and dotted lines	_____	E. a slow-moving river
6. wavy, with blonde highlights	_____	F. a mountain
7. meandering, with a calm surface	_____	G. a banana
8. winding and bumpy, with deep potholes	_____	H. agricultural countryside
9. hollow, with rough bark	_____	I. an application form

For reference, see the *Easier English Dictionary for Students* (0 7475 6624 0)

Emphasis & misunderstanding

A. (Emphasis) Match the sentences on the left with an appropriate sentence on the right.

1. The minister's *emphasis* on the word 'peace' was noticeable.

2. Our guide *accentuated* the importance of remaining calm if there was trouble.

3. Our teacher explained that it was *crucially important* to pace ourselves while revising for the exam.

4. At the People's Party conference, the *accent* was on youth unemployment.

5. *Prominent* trade unionists have called for a boycott of imported goods.

6. It is *of crucial importance* that we make more use of technology if we are to make progress.

A. The government will have to sit up and take note of what these *important* people have to say.

B. She *emphasised* the fact that panicking would only make matters worse.

C. The leader *gave prominence* to the need to create better job opportunities.

D. We consider progress in this field to be *extremely important.*

E. He *put great stress* on the maxim that 'All work and no play makes Jack a dull boy'.

F. He *stressed* again and again the importance of an established détente.

B. (Emphasis) Now complete these sentences with an expression in *bold* from the above exercise. In some cases, more than one answer may be possible.

1. Some medical treatments do very little to help the patient. In fact, in some cases, they only _____ the pain.

2. The revolution began when a _____ member of the ruling party was assassinated.

3. At the meeting of the Students' Council, the _____ was on better standards of accommodation.

4. She _____ the need to be fully prepared for all eventualities while travelling.

5. The Minister of Transport _____ on the need for an integrated transport policy.

6. It is _____ that we try to improve relations between our countries.

7. She banged the table for _____ as she spoke.

C. (Misunderstanding) Complete sentences 1 - 9 with an appropriate word or expression from the box. In some cases, more than one answer is possible.

| mix-up   •   obscure   •   impression   •   distorted |
| misapprehension • mistaken • confusion • assumed • confused |

1. She was _____ by the journalist's questions.

2. There were scenes of _____ at the airport when the snowstorm stopped all the flights.

3. We nearly didn't catch our flight because of a _____ over the tickets.

4. There are several _____ points in his letter. It's not very clear.

5. He _____ the meaning of my speech, creating the false impression that I was a racist.

6. He was under the _____ that socialism and communism were the same thing.

7. The jury _____ , wrongly, that he was innocent.

8. They were _____ in the belief that the refugees were in the country for economic rather than political reasons.

9. The press were under the _____ that the Prime Minister was about to resign.

For reference, see the *Easier English Dictionary for Students* (0 7475 6624 0)

Changes 2

A. Look at these sentences and decide if the statement which follows each one is <u>true</u> or <u>false</u>. Use the words and expressions in *bold* to help you decide.

1. The population of the country has trebled in the last 25 years.

   *There has been a **dramatic increase** in the number of people living in the country.*

2. Unemployment has dropped by about 2% every year for the last six years.

   *There has been a **steady decrease** in the number of people out of work.*

3. The government has spent a lot of money improving roads around the country.

   *There has been a **deterioration** in the national road system.*

4. The number of exam passes achieved by the school's pupils has risen by almost 50%.

   *There has been a **decline** in the number of exam passes.*

5. American travellers abroad have discovered that they can buy more foreign currency with their dollar.

   *There has been a **weakening** of the dollar.*

6. It is now much easier to import goods into the country than it was a few years ago.

   *There has been a **tightening up** of border controls.*

7. We're increasing our stocks of coal before the winter begins.

   *We're **running down** our stocks of coal.*

8. Prices have gone up by about 4% every year since 1998.

   *There has been a **constant rise** in the rate of inflation.*

9. The pass rate for the exam was 3% lower this year than it was last year.

   *There has been a **sharp fall** in the pass rate.*

10. The alliance are going to reduce the number of conventional weapons in their armed forces.

    *The alliance are going to **build up** the number of weapons they have.*

11. Deflation has adversely affected industries around the country.

    *There has been a **growth** in industrial activity.*

12. The rules are much stricter now than they were before.

    *There has been a **relaxation** of the rules.*

13. Last year, 12% of the population worked in industry and 10% worked in agriculture. This year, 14% of the population work in industry and 8% work in agriculture.

    *There has been a **narrowing of the gap** between those working in different sectors of the economy.*

For reference, see the *Easier English Dictionary for Students* (0 7475 6624 0)

14. Some management roles in the company will not exist this time next year.

    *Some management roles are going to be **phased out.***

15. More people are shopping at large supermarkets rather than small village shops.

    *There has been an **upward trend** in the number of people shopping in small village shops.*

16. Her English is clearly better now than it was when she first arrived.

    *There has been **marked progress** in her English.*

17. People live in better houses, drive nicer cars and eat higher-quality food than they did twenty years ago.

    *There has been a **general improvement** in the standard of living.*

18. Our company has opened factories in France, Germany and Italy in the last five years.

    *Our company has witnessed considerable **expansion** in the last five years.*

19. The government will spend less on the National Health Service next year.

    *There are going to be **cuts** in healthcare spending next year.*

20. British people nowadays want to see more of the world.

    *British people nowadays want to **narrow** their horizons.*

B. Check your answers, then use some of the words and expressions in bold above and in the answer key to write some sentences about your country.

_____

_____

_____

_____

_____

_____

_____

_____

_____

_____

_____

For reference, see the *Easier English Dictionary for Students* (0 7475 6624 0)

Opposites

Replace the words in *bold* in these sentences with a word from the box which has an opposite meaning.

VERBS

withdrew • fell • rewarded • loosened • refused (to let) • set
denied • deteriorated • abandoned • forbade • lowered
demolished • retreated • refused • simplified • defended • rejected

1. They *accepted* the offer of a ceasefire.

2. He *admitted* telling lies in his original statement.

3. The army slowly *advanced,* leaving a trail of devastation in its path.

4. They *agreed* to meet to discuss the future of the organisation.

5. The minister *attacked* his party's policies in a speech in Parliament.

6. The apartments blocks they *built* were the ugliest in the city.

7. He *complicated* matters by rewriting the original proposal.

8. They *continued with* their plans to assassinate the king when he opened the parliament.

9. He *deposited* £7,000 - half his college fees for the forthcoming year.

10. Relations between the two countries have *improved* considerably in the last year.

11. He *permitted* us to present our petition directly to the President.

12. The members of the commune were *punished* for their part in the revolution.

13. He *raised* the overall standards of the company within two months of his appointment.

14. As soon as the sun *rose,* the demonstrators began to appear on the streets.

15. Prices *rose* sharply in the first three months of the financial year.

16. As soon as he had *tightened* the knots, he pushed the boat out.

36

For reference, see the *Easier English Dictionary for Students* (0 7475 6624 0)

Opposites

ADJECTIVES

scarce	easy	approximate	dim	compulsory
delicate	innocent	detrimental	reluctant	crude
even	marked	graceful	clear	flexible

1. The meaning of his words was very **ambiguous**.

2. According to his colleagues, he's a very **awkward** person to deal with.

3. When she first started dancing, she was very **awkward.**

4. His policies were **beneficial** to the economy as a whole.

5. We need **exact** figures before we embark on a new venture.

6. The jury decided he was **guilty** of the crime.

7. Add up all the **odd** numbers between 1 and 20 to get a result.

8. Despite the weather, supplies of food after the harvest were **plentiful.**

9. The laws protecting the green belt around the city are very **rigid.**

10. There is a **slight** difference in the way the company is run these days compared with a few years ago.

11. The device is very **sophisticated** and should only be operated by someone who is familiar with it.

12. The spices used in the production of some international dishes have a very **strong** flavour.

13. The **strong** light from the torch picked out details on the walls of the cave.

14. Attendance at afternoon classes should be **voluntary.**

15. A lot of students are **willing** to attend classes on Saturday morning.

Don't forget to keep a record of the words and expressions that you have learnt, review your notes from time to time and try to use new vocabulary items whenever possible.

For reference, see the *Easier English Dictionary for Students* (0 7475 6624 0)

Addition, equation & conclusion

This module will help you to review more of the important words that we use to join ideas in an essay, a verbal presentation or sometimes in everyday speech (also see page 1 - *Condition* - and page 9 - *Contrast & comparison*).

A. Put the following words and expressions into their correct place in the table depending on their function.

to sum up briefly • it can be concluded that • also
similarly • likewise • besides • to conclude • too
in addition • in brief • in the same way • thus
what's more • furthermore • moreover • along with
to summarise • as well as • therefore • correspondingly

Addition (For example: and)	Equation (For example: equally)	Conclusion (For example: in conclusion)

B. Complete these sentences with one of the words or expressions from above. In most cases, more than one answer is possible.

1. Tourism brings much-needed money to developing countries. _____ , it provides employment for the local population.

2. _____ bringing much-needed money to developing countries, tourism provides employment for the local population.

3. Tourists should respect the local environment. _____ they should respect the local customs.

4. _____ industrial waste, pollution from car fumes is poisoning the environment.

5. In order to travel, you need a passport. _____ , you might need a visa, immunisation jabs and written permission to visit certain areas.

6. Drugs are banned in Britain - _____ weapons such as guns and knives.

7. All power corrupts. _____ , absolute power corrupts absolutely.

8. You shouldn't smoke, drink, take drugs or eat unhealthy food. _____ , you should live a more healthy lifestyle.

9. The ozone layer is becoming depleted, the air in the cities is becoming too dirty to breathe and our seas and rivers are no longer safe to swim in. _____ pollution is slowly destroying the planet.

10. Your grades have been very poor for the past two years. _____ you need to work really hard if you want to pass your exams next month.

For reference, see the *Easier English Dictionary for Students* (0 7475 6624 0)

Task commands

Look at the list of tasks in the first list. In particular, look at the words in *bold*, which are telling the writer/speaker what he/she must do. Match these words with a suitable definition of the task command in the second list. Two of these definitions can be used more than once.

1. *Account* for the increased use of technology in modern society. _____
2. *Analyse* the effects of climactic change around the world. _____
3. *Assess* the improvements you have made in your English since you started using this book. _____
4. *Compare* the lifestyles of young people in Britain and young people in your country. _____
5. *Define* the word 'hope'. _____
6. *Demonstrate* the different features of this computer. _____
7. *Discuss* the advantages and disadvantages of growing up in a single-parent family. _____
8. *Elaborate* on your feelings about capital punishment. _____
9. *Estimate* the costs of setting up a website for the company. _____
10. *Evaluate* how useful our class visit to the Bank of England was. _____
11. *Examine* the causes of global warming. _____
12. *Explain* the sudden interest in old-fashioned toys such as yo-yos. _____
13. *Identify* the person who attacked you. _____
14. *Illustrate* the problems the National Health Service is currently facing. _____
15. *Justify* your reasons for refusing to help me. _____
16. *Outline* the history of the motor car in the last fifty years. _____
17. *Predict* the changes that we are going to see in information technology in the next ten years. _____
18. *Suggest* ways in which you can become a more efficient student. _____
19. *Summarise* your feelings towards a united Europe. _____
20. *Trace* the development of nuclear technology from its earliest days. _____

A. Describe what you think can be done in order to achieve something.
B. Tell in advance what you think will happen.
C. Explain, with real examples, why something has happened or is happening.
D. Give a brief history of something, in the order in which it happened.
E. Give the meaning of something.
F. Talk about something with someone else, or write about it from different viewpoints.
G. Calculate (but not exactly) the value or cost of something.
H. Give a broad description of something without giving too much detail.
I. Explain something closely and scientifically.
J. Write or talk about the different aspects (e.g., causes, results) of something.
K. Explain something in more detail than you did previously.
L. Look at two things side by side to see how they are similar or different.
M. Explain something in a few main points, without giving too much detail.
N. Say why something has happened.
O. Show or prove that something is right or good.
P. Show how something works, usually by physically operating it so that the other person knows what it does and how it works.
Q. Give a physical description of somebody.
R. Calculate the value of something.

For reference, see the *Easier English Dictionary for Students* (0 7475 6624 0)

Confusing words & false friends

CONFUSING WORDS

Confusing words are two or more words which have a similar meaning to each other but are used in a different way.

OR

Are related to the same topic, but have a different meaning.

OR

Look similar, but have a different meaning.

FALSE FRIENDS

False friends are words in English which have a similar-looking word in another language but which have a different meaning.

Complete the following sentences with the appropriate word.

1. *action / activity*

   The police took immediate _____ when they realised the situation was getting out of hand.

   Economic _____ stagnated as the recession took hold.

2. *advice / advise*

   Can you _____ me on the best course of action to take?

   He offered me some excellent _____ .

3. *affect / effect*

   Cuts in spending will have a serious _____ on the National Health Service.

   The strike will seriously _____ train services.

4. *appreciable / appreciative*

   There is an _____ difference between manslaughter and murder.

   She was very _____ of our efforts to help.

5. *assumption / presumption*

   They raised taxes on the _____ that it would help control spending.

   It's sheer _____ for the government to suggest things have improved since they came to power.

6. *avoid / prevent*

   Rapid government reforms managed to _____ a revolution taking place.

   He's always trying to _____ taking a decision if he can help it.

7. *beside / besides*

   The office is just _____ the railway station.

   _____ their regular daytime job, many people do extra work in the evening.

For reference, see the *Easier English Dictionary for Students* (0 7475 6624 0)

Confusing words & false friends

8. *briefly / shortly*

_____ before the conflict began, the army pulled down the border posts.

The minister spoke _____ about the need for political reform.

9. *channel / canal*

The television _____ received a formal complaint about the programme.

The Suez _____ was built in the second half of the nineteenth century.

10. *conscientious / conscious*

Most people are _____ of the need to protect the environment.

_____ workers should be rewarded for their hard work.

11. *continual / continuous*

A _____ trade embargo has badly affected the economic infrastructure.

The computer has given us _____ problems ever since we installed it.

12. *control / inspect*

Environmental health officers regularly _____ kitchens and other food preparation areas.

The government plans to _____ the price of meat to make sure it doesn't go up too much.

13 *criticism(s) / objection(s)*

They didn't raise any _____ when we insisted on inspecting the figures.

The government's plan was met with severe _____ .

14. *damage / injury / harm*

It was a severe _____ which needed immediate hospital treatment.

A lot of _____ was caused to buildings along the coast during the storm.

There's no _____ in taking a break from your job now and then.

15. *discover / invent*

When did he _____ the telephone?

Did Alexander Fleming _____ penicillin?

For reference, see the *Easier English Dictionary for Students* (0 7475 6624 0)

Confusing words & false friends

16. *during / for / while*

Shops were closed _____ the duration of the conflict.

_____ the transition from a dictatorship to democracy, the country experienced severe strikes and riots.

The bomb went off _____ the President was making his speech.

17. *however / moreover*

The plan was good in theory. _____ , in practice it was extremely difficult to implement.

The plan was excellent. _____ , it was clear from the beginning that it was going to be a success.

18. *inconsiderate / inconsiderable*

An _____ amount of money was wasted.

_____ behaviour makes life unpleasant for everybody.

19. *intolerable / intolerant*

I consider his behaviour to be quite _____ .

The government is _____ of other political parties.

20. *job / work*

Everybody has the right to a decent _____ with good pay.

Following the recession, many people are still looking for _____ .

21. *lay(s) / lie(s)*

The city of Quito _____ near the equator.

The manager made it clear he intended to _____ down some strict rules.

22. *look at / watch*

We must _____ the situation in Lugumba carefully, and be prepared to act if violence flares again.

We need to _____ the problem carefully and decide if there is anything we can do about it.

23. *permission / permit*

I'm afraid we can't _____ photography in here.

They received _____ to attend the sessions as long as they didn't interrupt.

For reference, see the *Easier English Dictionary for Students* (0 7475 6624 0)

Confusing words & false friends

24. possibility / chance

There is always the _____ that the government will reverse its decision.

If we act now, we have a good _____ of finding a cure for the disease.

25. practise / practice

It's important to _____ your English whenever possible.

You need more _____ before you take the exam.

26. priceless / worthless

_____ paintings by artists like Van Gogh should not be in the hands of private collectors.

As inflation spiralled out of control, paper money suddenly became _____ .

27. principal(s) / principle(s)

Many people refuse to eat meat on _____ .

The _____ of the college is an ardent non-smoker.

The country's _____ products are paper and wood.

Not many people are familiar with the _____ of nuclear physics.

28. process / procession

The _____ made its way down the avenue.

Applying for a visa can be a long and frustrating _____ .

29. raise / rise

As prices _____ , demand usually drops.

In response to the current oil shortage, most airlines plan to _____ their fares.

30. respectable / respectful

The delegates listened in _____ silence as the chairman spoke.

They want to bring up their children in an area which is considered to be _____ .

31. treat / cure

Hospitals are so understaffed that they find it almost impossible to _____ patients with minor injuries.

They were unable to _____ the disease, and hundreds died as a result.

For reference, see the *Easier English Dictionary for Students* (0 7475 6624 0)

Useful interview expressions

Below you will see some common expressions that you might find useful in the IELTS speaking test. Put each expression into the correct box according to the function of that expression.

1. May I think about that for a moment?
2. In short,...
3. What I'm trying to say is...
4. To sum up,...
5. What are your views on...?
6. Would you mind repeating that?
7. How can I put this?
8. In other words...
9. Sorry to butt in...
10. Well, as a matter of fact...
11. I'm not so sure about that
12. Pardon?
13. I can't help thinking the same

14. What are your feelings about...?
15. So in conclusion,...
16. I see things rather differently myself
17. True enough
18. That's right
19. I don't entirely agree with you
20. Perhaps I should make that clearer by saying...
21. How can I best say this?
22. Could you repeat what you said?
23. I couldn't agree more
24. Actually...

25. To put it another way...
26. That's just what I was thinking
27. In brief,...
28. Could I just say that...
29. Well, my own opinion is that...
30. That's my view exactly
31. To summarise,...
32. What was that?
33. I must take issue with you on that
34. Let me get this right
35. Sorry to interrupt, but....
36. I'm afraid I didn't catch that
37. What's your opinion?

Agreeing with somebody	Disagreeing with somebody
Example: Yes, I agree.	Example: I'm afraid I disagree.

Interrupting	Asking for clarification or repetition
Example: Excuse me for interrupting.	Example: I'm sorry?

Asking somebody for their opinion	Saying something in another way
Example: What do you think about...?	Example: What I mean is.....

Giving yourself time to think	Summing up
Example: (in response to a question) Let me see.	Example: So basically.....

For reference, see the *Easier English Dictionary for Students* (0 7475 6624 0)

Complete the following phrasal verbs with a preposition(s) or particle(s) from the box. The meaning of the phrasal verb is given in brackets at the end of each sentence.

over	•	back	•	into	•	forward	•	of
on	•	down	•	to	•	up	•	behind
out	•	in	•	off	•	with

1. Some parents are criticized for the way they **bring** _____ their children. *(raise)*

2. The committee members **fell** _____ over plans for the new health centre. *(argued)*

3. They refused to **face** _____ _____ their responsibilities, with disastrous consequences. *(accept an unpleasant state of affairs, and try to deal with it)*

4. The President decided to **call** _____ his visit to Europe. *(not to go ahead with something)*

5. It is only at election time that Members of Parliament **count** _____ support from their constituents. *(rely / depend)*

6. Many developing countries are failing to **catch** _____ _____ their more developed neighbours. *(get to the same level)*

7. It can take months or even years for political scandals to **die** _____. *(become less strong)*

8. An alarming number of students **drop** _____ _____ school early every year. *(leave)*

9. Major international companies can't **figure** _____ the popularity of the anti-capitalist movement. *(find it hard to understand)*

10. If they examined the issues more closely, they would **find** _____ the reasons for the changes. *(discover)*

11. As we **grow** _____ our priorities change. *(change from being children to being adults),*

12. Students can be quite creative with the reasons they give for not **handing** _____ their homework. *(giving their teachers)*

13. Salaries very rarely **keep** _____ _____ the cost of living. *(rise at the same speed as)*

14. The latest Avicenna report **leaves** _____ the reasons for demographic shifts. *(does not include)*

15. It does **point** _____ the mistakes made by the agency over the last few years. *(show)*

16. Before you write your essay, you should **look** _____ the Party's history. *(research)*

17. Many employees **carried** _____ working despite pressure from the unions. *(continued)*

18. Once people **fall** _____ with their mortgage payments, they come under extreme financial pressure from their bank. *(become late)*

19. The first step to a healthier lifestyle is to **cut** _____ _____ the number of cigarettes you smoke each day. *(reduce)*

20. It is becoming more common for people to **cut** _____ meat from their diet. *(stop eating)*

21. During the 1990's, a lot of hospitals were **taken** _____ by private trusts. *(become controlled by another organisation)*

22. When computer technology fails us, we have to **make do** _____ more primitive methods. They're called 'pen and paper'. *(use something because there is nothing else available)*

23. In this essay, I'd like to **put** _____ the arguments in favour of global capitalism. *(suggest or state the case for something)*

24. When I **look** _____ _____ my childhood, I remember the many sacrifices my parents made for me. *(think about something that happened in the past)*

For reference, see the *Easier English Dictionary for Students* (0 7475 6624 0)

Phrasal verbs 2

Complete the second sentence in each pair with a phrasal verb from the box so that it has the same meaning as the first sentence. You will need to change the verb form in most of the sentences.

break down •	carry out •	cut back on •	cut off •	do away with
do up •	end up •	fall through •	hold up •	keep on
let down •	let off •	pull out of •	pull through •	show up
sort out •	split up •	wear off •	wear out •	work out

1. Peace talks between the two countries collapsed when neither side reached an agreement.

   Peace talks between the two countries _____ when neither side reached an agreement.

2. I'm trying to calculate if we've sold more this year than last year.

   I'm trying to _____ if we've sold more this year than last year.

3. The effects of the drug disappear after a few hours.

   The effects of the drug _____ after a few hours.

4. A lot of people exhaust themselves through overwork.

   A lot of people _____ themselves _____ through overwork.

5. Despite the severity of the disease, many people recover with the help of appropriate drugs.

   Despite the severity of the disease, many people _____ with the help of appropriate drugs.

6. Through careful negotiation, they were able to resolve the problem.

   Through careful negotiation, they were able to _____ the problem.

7. When parents start to live apart, it can be particularly difficult for their children to cope.

   When parents _____ , it can be particularly difficult for their children to cope.

8. At the opening night, only a few audience members came.

   At the opening night, only a few audience members _____ .

9. The Australian partners stopped being a part of the deal at the last moment.

   The Australian partners _____ the deal at the last moment.

10. People celebrate the Chinese New Year by exploding fireworks in the street.

    People celebrate the Chinese New Year by _____ fireworks in the street.

For reference, see the *Easier English Dictionary for Students* (0 7475 6624 0)

11. It is pointless relying on people to help you if they don't do as they promised.

It is pointless relying on people to help you if they _____ you _____.

12. New government pension plans mean that many people will continue working well into their seventies.

New government pension plans mean that many people will _____ working well into their seventies.

13. The planned changes were delayed because committee members argued among themselves.

The planned changes were _____ because committee members argued among themselves.

14. At the last minute, the plans for the proposed motorway didn't take place.

At the last minute, the plans for the proposed motorway _____ .

15. During the recession, many workers in the primary sector became jobless.

During the recession, many workers in the primary sector _____ jobless.

16. Doctors did some tests on the patients.

Doctors _____ some tests on the patients.

17. Minor economies, such as spending less on staff costs, can often prevent a company sliding into bankruptcy.

Minor economies, such as _____ staff costs, can often prevent a company sliding into bankruptcy.

18. We were accidentally disconnected in the middle of our phone call.

We were accidentally _____ in the middle of our phone call.

19. Once the government removed quotas, the market was flooded with cheap foreign imports.

Once the government _____ quotas, the market was flooded with cheap foreign imports.

20. It cost almost £8 million to renovate the stadium, by which time the team was in serious financial difficulties.

It cost almost £8 million to _____ the stadium, by which time the team was in serious financial difficulties.

For reference, see the *Easier English Dictionary for Students* (0 7475 6624 0)

Phrasal verbs 3

These sentences can all be completed with a phrasal verb using *come* or *get*. In one case, either may be possible. Make sure you use the correct form of the verb in each one.

1. In rural districts, it can be difficult to _____ by without a car.

2. Scientists _____ across the cure by accident, while studying the health benefits of a rare species of plant.

3. The anti-smoking message is finally _____ through to people.

4. Large industries can no longer _____ away with dumping industrial waste in rivers.

5. Doctors realised there was going to be a problem when several people in the same village _____ down with suspected food poisoning.

6. It can be very difficult to _____ down to studying for exams when the weather is nice.

7. It was only after he _____ into his inheritance after his father died that he was able to expand the company.

8. After the revolution, it took almost five years for the country to _____ round to opening its borders.

9. The government _____ up against a lot of opposition from locals when they proposed building an immigration centre near the village.

10. Developed countries are usually able to _____ through a period of recession by drawing on financial reserves.

11. There was strong resistance to the union when it urged workers to _____ out on strike.

12. People who live in close proximity to one another must learn to _____ on with their neighbours.

13. Nothing _____ of the company's plans to develop solar-powered vehicles.

14. The final bill for the project _____ to almost £10 million.

15. For most poor people, _____ out of the cycle of poverty can be next to impossible.

16. In any dispute with an insurance company, it is usually the consumer who _____ off the worst.

17. When supply of a particular product exceeds demand, it is common for the price to _____ down.

18. By the time the message _____ through it was too late to evacuate the residents.

19. The country never _____ over the effects of the civil war.

20. Generally, people are reluctant to break rules, but will try to _____ round them somehow.

Phrasal verbs 4

The following sentences all use phrasal verbs with *give*, *go* or *look*. However, half of them use the wrong phrasal verb. Decide which ones are wrong and replace them with the correct phrasal verb, which you will find in the other sentences.

1. I'd like you to **look after** these figures and tell me if you think the project is possible.

2. As ticket prices **go up**, fewer people go to the cinema and prefer to stay at home with a video.

3. People who have to **give in** elderly relatives or other dependants should receive financial support.

4. The chancellor had decided to stand firm on his decision, but under pressure from protesters, he decided to **go into** and reduce tax on petrol.

5. The committee were asked to **look into** the latest crime statistics and try to establish a pattern.

6. It is important not to let the fire **go out**, as it's the main source of power.

7. Very few children **give off** their end-of-year school exams.

8. The threat of severe reprisals meant that many refused to **give** themselves **up** to the police.

9. Before entering an agreement, it is essential to **go off** the details very carefully.

10. People who want to know how to **go about** starting their own company should talk to a trained adviser.

11. Some people tend to **go over** others who are less fortunate purely because of their financial situation.

12. There were very few clues to the crime, and police didn't have enough information to **go on**.

13. People often **look over** the idea of starting their own company when they realise the risks that are involved.

14. Even if you fail the first time, you should **go on** trying.

15. After years of decline, government investment is revitalising the area, and things are beginning to **look up**.

16. The first step to a healthier lifestyle is to **give up** smoking.

17. New legislation lays down strict penalties for factories which **look up** to poisonous fumes.

18. We decided not to **go through** with our plans until we had sufficient capital.

19. Although children should **look forward** to their parents, many rebel against their values and way of life.

20. We asked them for more information, but they refused to **look down** on details.

For reference, see the *Easier English Dictionary for Students* (0 7475 6624 0)

Phrasal verbs 5

The verbs and particles in the two boxes can be combined to make phrasal verbs, which can then be used to complete the sentences below.

Decide which phrasal verbs go into each sentence, and write the answers in the crossword grid. In many cases, you will need to change the form of the verb (eg, past participle, infinitive, third person 's', etc). The meaning of each phrasal verb is in italics at the end of each sentence.

Don't forget that some phrasal verbs need two particles.

The first one has been done as an example.

talk	put	take	run	turn
opt	stand	pick	make	set

on	off	with	for
round	against	down	aside
in	out	up	after

Clues across (➡)

1. Accommodation in some cities is so expensive that some people cannot even afford to _____ the 8 weeks' deposit that is required. *(to make a deposit)* **Answer = put down**

4. They were reluctant to make changes, but we managed to _____ them _____. *(to persuade somebody)*

5. Children often _____ one of their parents, either in their mannerisms or in the way they look. *(to resemble)*

6. After _____ a few unexpected difficulties, they decided to scrap the project. *(to stop because something is in the way)*

8. They were _____ of the apartment by their landlord when they could no longer afford the rent, and ended up living on the street. *(to be forced to leave)*

11. When I was at school, some teachers unfairly _____ children who avoided sport because they prefered more creative interests and pastimes. *(to choose someone to attack or criticize)*

12. Although many companies offer their employees a pension programme, many decide to _____ of the programme and make their own arrangements. *(to decide not to take part in something)*

16. A lot of applicants expressed an interest in the job, but only a handful _____ for the interview. *(to arrive for a meeting, appointment, etc)*

19. Air pollution can _____ asthma and other chest diseases in those most vulnerable. *(to start)*

20. People who use credit cards unwisely can easily _____ debts of thousands of pounds every month. *(to make debts go up quickly)*

21. By the time he was 18, he had _____ his mind that he wanted to be famous. *(to decide on something)*

Clues down (⬇)

1. It's often a good idea to _____ some money for a 'rainy day'. *(to save money)*

2. Technology is moving at such a fast pace it is no longer possible to _____ all the latest developments. *(to understand or assimilate information)*

3. Nobody was _____ by the government's false figures on unemployment. *(to be fooled or tricked)*

5. He _____ the job that was offered to him, even though he was desperate for the money. *(to refuse something which is offered)*

7. Most people will _____ a stressful job if the money is good enough. *(to tolerate something which is not very pleasant)*

9. He was unable to make the speech, so I was asked to _____ and make it on his behalf. *(to take the place of someone - often also used with 'for')*

10. A lot of people are _____ the idea of working for themselves because of the lack of a regular salary. *(to be discouraged from doing something, usually because of a potentially negative outcome)*

13. Once bad weather _____, people tend to stay at home rather than go out. *(to start and become permanent)*

14. Doctors amd medical experts were unable to _____ why some people survived the virus and others didn't. *(to understand or know the reason for something)*

15. She _____ a story about ghosts in the cellar to stop us going down there, but of course we didn't believe her. *(to invent a story)*

17. At the age of 38 he _____ the post of President, but lacked sufficient experience to be taken seriously. *(to apply for a job in politics, competing against other people for the same job)*

18. Despite massive promotion by the tourist board. it took a long time for tourism to _____ again after the terrorist attacks. *(to improve, to get better)*

For reference, see the *Easier English Dictionary for Students* (0 7475 6624 0)

Spelling

A. There are several words in this passage which are spelt incorrectly. Can you find and correct them?

Apart from condemming tobacco companies and rising the price of cigarettes, the goverment's anti-smoking campain has failed to have any long-term affects, and the only people bennefitting from it are the Inland Revenue departement. Meanwhile, persistant smokers are being denied treatment by the NHS.

	These words are spelt incorrectly	These are the correct spellings
1.		
2.		
3.		
4.		
5.		
6.		
7.		
8.		

B. Instructions as above.

It is argueable whether good pronounciation is more important than good grammer and vocabulery. Consientious students balance their aquisition of these skills, hopeing to acheive both fluency and accuracey. Teachers should encourage there students to practice all the relevant language skills.

	These words are spelt incorrectly	These are the correct spellings
1.		
2.		
3.		
4.		
5.		
6.		
7.		
8.		
9.		

For reference, see the *Easier English Dictionary for Students* (0 7475 6624 0)

10.		
11.		

C. Instructions as per previous page

It is becomming increasingly difficcult for many to find decent acommodation in London at a price they can afford. To put it simpley, most people just don't have the neccesary funds. Organiseations such as Home Front can offer advise, but it widely agreed that the situation is no longer managable. The fact that city councils are building cheap, tempory housing for lower-paid profesionals is the only official acknowledgment of this problem.

	These words are spelt incorrectly	These are the correct spellings
1.		
2.		
3.		
4.		
5.		
6.		
7.		
8.		
9.		
10.		
11.		

For reference, see the *Easier English Dictionary for Students* (0 7475 6624 0)

Education

A. Look at the sentences below and fill in the gaps using the appropriate word from A, B or C.

1. He didn't get a good grade the first time he did his IELTS exam, so decided to _____ it.
       A. resit   *B. remake*   *C. repair*

2. People who attend university later in life are often called _____ students.
       A. aged   *B. mature*   *C. old*

3. Although she had left school and was working, she went to evening classes at the local College of _____ Education.
       A. Upper   *B. Further*   *C. Higher*

4. After he left school, he decided to go on to _____ education and applied for a place at Edinburgh University.
       A. further   *B. upper*   *C. higher*

5. He received a local government _____ to help him pay for his course.
       A. fee   *B. fare*   *C. grant*

6. Education helps us to acquire knowledge and learn new _____ .
       A. skills   *B. powers*   *C. abilities*

7. Although she already had a first degree from university, she decided that she wanted to work towards a _____ degree later in life.
       A. further   *B. senior*   *C. higher*

8. We should make the best of every _____ to learn.
       A. chance   *B. opportunity*   *C. availability*

9. Nowadays, _____ education is promoted a lot in schools.
       A. body   *B. health*   *C. vitality*

10. A large number of parents are dissatisfied with the _____ education system, and put their children into private schools instead.
       A. government   *B. national*   *C. state*

11. Because so many students find exams stressful, some colleges offer a system of _____ assessment instead.
       A. continual   *B. continuous*   *C. continuing*

12. He has read a lot of books and _____ a lot of knowledge.
       A. acquired   *B. won*   *C. achieved*

B. Complete sentences 1-11 with a suitable word or expression from the box.

primary • numeracy • graduate • evening class • course				
discipline • literacy • day release • kindergarten • enrol				
secondary • skills • pass • correspondence • qualifications • degree				

1. When Michael was three, he started going to a _____ .

2. At the age of five, he entered _____ education.

3. He learned basic _____ such as _____ and _____ .

For reference, see the *Easier English Dictionary for Students* (0 7475 6624 0)

Education

4. After he turned eleven he began to attend _____ school.

5. Although he was lazy and lacked sufficient _____ , he was able to _____ his exams.

6. When he was eighteen he found a college which offered a _____ in Art and Design.

7. He was able to _____ for the course a few days before his nineteenth birthday.

8. He worked hard and three years later was able to _____ with a _____ in Art and Design.

9. After that he followed a _____ course in photography from a college in the USA using the Internet.

10. The _____ he gained impressed an advertising company he wanted to work for.

11. Although he is now working, he has decided to attend an _____ after work, although he was disappointed that his boss didn't offer him _____ .

C. Now read this essay and complete the gaps with one of the words or expressions from Tasks A and B. You may need to change the form of some of the words.

'You are never too old to learn'. Do you agree with this statement?

Education is a long process that not only provides us with basic (1)_____ such as (2)_____ and (3)_____ , but is also essential in shaping our future lives. From the moment we enter (4)_____ as small children, and as we progress through (5)_____ and (6)_____ education, we are laying the foundations for the life ahead of us. We must (7)_____ ourselves to work hard so that we can (8)_____ exams and gain the (9)_____ we will need to secure a good job. We must also (10)_____ valuable life skills so that we can fit in and work with those around us. And of course (11)_____ education helps us to understand how we can stay fit and healthy.

For most people, this process ends when they are in their mid-to-late teens. For others, however, it is the beginning of a lifetime of learning. After they finish school, many progress to (12)_____ education where they will learn more useful skills such as computer literacy or basic business management. Others will (13)_____ on a programme of (14)_____ education at a university where, with hard work, they will have the opportunity to (15)_____ after three or four years with a well-earned (16)_____ . After that, they may work for a while before opting to study for a (17)_____ degree - an MA, for example, or a PhD. Alternatively, they may choose to attend an (18)_____ after work or, if they have a sympathetic employer, obtain (19)_____ so that they can study during the week. And if they live a long way from a college or university, they might follow a (20)_____ course using mail and the Internet. In fact, it is largely due to the proliferation of computers that many people who have not been near a school for many years, have started to study again and can proudly class themselves as (21)_____ students.

We live in a fascinating and constantly changing world, and we must continually learn and acquire new knowledge if we are to adapt and keep up with changing events. Our schooldays are just the beginning of this process, and we should make the best of every (22) _____ to develop ourselves, whether we are eighteen or eighty. You are, indeed, never too old to learn.

For reference, see the *Easier English Dictionary for Students* (0 7475 6624 0)

The media

A. Match the words and expressions in box A with a suitable definition in box B.

Box A.

1. current affairs	**2.** reporters	**3.** journalists	**4.** tabloids
5. broadsheets	**6.** coverage	**7.** information overload	**8.** broadcasts
9. web	**10.** website	**11.** download	**12.** the Internet **13.** log on

Box B.

A. large-format newspapers

B. small-format newspapers

C. people who write for newspapers or periodicals

D. the amount of space or time given to an event in newspapers or on television

E. the political situation as it is now

F. radio or television programmes

G. to enter a password and start to access a computer system

H. journalists who write reports of events for a newspaper, periodical or television programme

I. the millions of pages and sites which display text and images within the Internet

J. to transfer pages from a web site onto your own computer

K. the international network linking millions of computers

L. a modern expression referring to the inability of a human to process everything he or she hears and sees

M. a collection of related pages on the World Wide Web created by a company, organisation or individual

B. Complete this extract from a television interview with an appropriate word or expression from the box.

entertainment • invasion of privacy • exploiting • libel • censorship
information • readership • media tycoon • paparazzi • freedom of the press
unscrupulous • gutter press • chequebook journalism

Interviewer: Welcome to today's programme. Today we will be discussing the 1_____ , and asking the question: Should we allow newspapers and television channels to print or say whatever they like? In the studio I have television personality Timothy Blake and 2_____ Rupert Poubelle, multi-millionaire owner of the Daily Views newspaper. Timothy, let's start with you.

T.B.: Thank you. In my opinion, it's time the government imposed stricter 3_____ of the press in order to prevent 4_____ journalists and reporters from making money by 5_____ people. I have often accused Mr Poubelle's organisation of 6_____ - nowadays I can't even sunbathe in my garden without being photographed by his hordes of 7_____ . They're like vultures. And everything they print about me is lies, complete rubbish.

Interviewer: But isn't it true that the media provides us with valuable 8_____

For reference, see the *Easier English Dictionary for Students* (0 7475 6624 0)

and 9_____ , and censorship would deprive us of much of this? Rupert?

R.P.: Of course. Mr. Blake's accusations are unfounded, as are the accusations of 10_____ we have received, but I can safely say that my journalists never pay people money to create stories. We are simply reporting the truth. Of course, if Mr. Blake wants to sue us for 11_____ , he is very welcome to try. But he would be depriving our 12_____ - all eight million of them - of the things they want...

T.B.: You're talking rubbish, as usual, like the pathetic 13_____ you own and use to fill your pockets with dirty money.

R.P.: Now look here, mate...

C. Now read this essay and complete the gaps with one of the words or expressions from Tasks A and B. You may need to change the form of some of the words.

'The media plays a valuable role in keeping us informed and entertained. However, many people believe it has too much power and freedom.' Discuss your views on this, giving examples and presenting a balanced argument both in favour of, and against, the power and freedom of the media.

Barely a hundred years ago, if we wanted to stay informed about what was going on in the world, we had to rely on word of mouth or, at best, newspapers. But because communication technology was very basic, the news we received was often days or weeks old.

We still have newspapers, of course, but they have changed almost beyond recognition. Whether we choose to read the 1_____ , with their quality 2_____ of news and other 3_____ by top 4_____ and articles by acclaimed 5_____ , or if we prefer the popular 6_____ , with their lively gossip and colourful stories, we are exposed to a wealth of information barely conceivable at the beginning of the last century.

We also have television and radio. News 7_____ let us know about world events practically as they happen, while sitcoms, chat shows and documentaries, etc. keep us entertained and informed. And there is also the 8_____ , where we can access information from millions of 9_____ around the world which we can then 10_____ onto our own computers.

However, these forms of 11_____ and 12_____ (or 'infotainment' as they are now sometimes collectively called) have their negative side. Famous personalities frequently accuse the 13_____ (and sometimes even respectable papers) of 14_____ by the 15_____ who are determined to get a story at any cost. Newspapers are often accused of 16_____ by angry politicians who dislike reading lies about themselves, and there are frequent accusations of 17_____ , with 18_____ reporters paying people to create stories for their newspapers or television programmes. Of course, it is not just the papers which are to blame. Sex and violence are increasing on the television. Undesirable people fill the 19_____ with equally undesirable material which can be accessed by anyone with a home computer. And the fear of 20_____ prevents many from 21_____ to the Internet.

Many argue that the government should impose stricter 22_____ to prevent such things happening. But others argue that 23_____ is the keystone of a free country. Personally, I take the view that while the media may occasionally abuse its position of power, the benefits greatly outweigh the disadvantages. Our lives would be much emptier without the wealth of information available to us today, and we are better people as a result.

For reference, see the *Easier English Dictionary for Students* (0 7475 6624 0)

Work

A. How would you generally feel, happy ☺ or unhappy ☹ , if you were in the following situations. Use the words in bold to help you decide.

1. The company you work for is well-known for its **job security.** ☺ ☹

2. You were suddenly **made redundant.** ☺ ☹

3. You received a **promotion.** ☺ ☹

4. You were given an **increment.** ☺ ☹

5. You worked **unsociable hours.** ☺ ☹

6. You had a **steady job.** ☺ ☹

7. You had **adverse working conditions.** ☺ ☹

8. You suddenly found yourself **unemployed.** ☺ ☹

9. You took time off work because of **repetitive strain injury.** ☺ ☹

10. The office where you work has **sick building syndrome.** ☺ ☹

11. You receive regular **perks** as part of your job. ☺ ☹

12. Somebody called you a **workaholic.** ☺ ☹

13. Your company doesn't give you many **incentives.** ☺ ☹

14. Your boss announces that there is going to be some **downsizing** of the workforce. ☺ ☹

15. Your work didn't offer much **job satisfaction.** ☺ ☹

16. Your company has a generous **incentive scheme.** ☺ ☹

17. You receive a **commission** for the work you have done. ☺ ☹

18. You receive support from a **union.** ☺ ☹

19. You were under **stress.** ☺ ☹

20. You were forced to **resign.** ☺ ☹

21. You received a cut in your **salary.** ☺ ☹

22. Your company gave you **sickness benefit.** ☺ ☹

23. You found your job very **demanding.** ☺ ☹

For reference, see the *Easier English Dictionary for Students* (0 7475 6624 0)

B. Match sentences 1-6 in box A with one of the sentences A-F in box B. Use the words in bold to help you.

Box A.

1. Samantha is the assistant manager of a bank and she works from 8.30 to 5.30 every day.

2. Tracy works on the production line of a factory which makes cars. She uses a machine to spray paint onto the finished car parts.

3. Jane works for herself. She is a photographer. She works every day for about eight or nine hours.

4. Jeanette is a cleaner for a company in Birmingham, but she only works there for about three or four hours a day.

5. Claire has a powerful job in the personnel office of a large multinational company. She is responsible for employing new people and getting rid of those that the company doesn't want to employ any more.

6. Marie works in the finance department of an international college in Oxford.

Box B.

A. She is a *semi-skilled blue-collar worker* in a *manufacturing industry*.

B. She is a *self-employed* and works *full-time.* She likes to describe herself as *freelance*.

C. She is responsible for *hiring and firing.*

D. She calculates the *wages, salaries, pension contributions* and *medical insurance contributions* of all the staff.

E. She is a *full-time white-collar worker* in a *service industry.*

F. She is an *unskilled part-time employee*.

Don't forget to keep a record of the words and expressions that you have learnt, review your notes from time to time and try to use new vocabulary items whenever possible.

For reference, see the *Easier English Dictionary for Students* (0 7475 6624 0)

Work

C. Now read this essay and complete the gaps with one of the words or expressions from Tasks A and B. You may need to change the form of some of the words.

'Some people live to work, and others work to live. In most cases, this depends on the job they have and the conditions under which they are employed. In your opinion, what are the elements that make a job worthwhile?'

In answering this question, I would like to look first at the elements that combine to make a job undesirable. By avoiding such factors, potential 1_____ are more likely to find a job that is more worthwhile, and by doing so, hope to achieve happiness in their work.

First of all, it doesn't matter if you are an 2_____ worker cleaning the floor, a 3_____ 4_____ worker on a production line in one of the 5_____ , or a 6_____ worker in a bank, shop or one of the other 7_____ : if you lack 8_____ , with the knowledge that you might lose your job at any time, you will never feel happy. Everybody would like a 9_____ in which he or she is guaranteed work. Nowadays, however, companies have a high turnover of staff, 10_____ new staff and 11_____ others on a weekly basis. Such companies are not popular with their workers.

The same can be said of a job in which you are put under a lot of 12_____ and worry, a job which is so 13_____ that it takes over your life, a job where you work 14_____ and so never get to see your family or friends, or a physical job in which you do the same thing every day and end up with the industrial disease that is always in the papers nowadays - 15_____ .

With all these negative factors, it would be difficult to believe that there are any elements that make a job worthwhile. Money is, of course, the prime motivator, and everybody wants a good 16_____ . But of course that is not all. The chance of 17_____ , of being given a better position in a company, is a motivating factor. Likewise, 18_____ such as a free lunch or a company car, an 19_____ scheme to make you work hard such as a regular 20_____ above the rate of inflation, 21_____ in case you fall ill and a company 22_____ scheme so that you have some money when you retire all combine to make a job worthwhile.

Unfortunately, it is not always easy to find all of these. There is, however, an alternative. Forget the office and the factory floor and become 23_____ and work for yourself. Your future may not be secure, but at least you will be happy.

> *Don't forget to keep a record of the words and expressions that you have learnt, review your notes from time to time and try to use new vocabulary items whenever possible.*

For reference, see the *Easier English Dictionary for Students* (0 7475 6624 0)

Money & finance

A. Use a dictionary to find the differences between the words and expressions in *bold* in the following groups.

1. make *a profit* & make *a loss*
2. *extravagant* & *frugal / economical*
3. a *current account* & a *deposit account*
4. a *loan* & a *mortgage*
5. to *deposit* money & to *withdraw money*
6. a *wage* & a *salary*
7. *broke* & *bankrupt*
8. *shares, stocks,* and *dividends*
9. *income tax* & *excise duty*
10. to *credit* & to *debit*

11. a *bank* and a *building society*
12. a *discount* & a *refund*
13. something which was a *bargain*, something which was *overpriced* and something which was *exorbitant*
14. *worthless* & *priceless*
15. *save money* and *invest money*
16. *inflation* and *deflation*
17. *income* and *expenditure*
18. to *lend* and to *borrow*

B. Match the sentences in column A with the sentences in column B. Use the words in *bold* to help you.

Column A	Column B
1. The managing director believes the company should start producing pocket computers.	A. I'm really looking forward to spending my *pension.*
2. I always put my money in a building society and not in a bank.	B. The *cost of living* seems to go up every day.
3. I can't afford to buy a new car right now. I don't have enough money.	C. Of course, it's always so difficult to *economise.*
4. I find Christmas a very expensive time.	D. Shops all over the country are making huge *reductions* on just about everything.
5. I came into a lot of money recently when my uncle died.	E. I always seem to run up a huge *overdraft* at the bank.
6. Look at this cheque that came in the post this morning from the Inland Revenue.	F. Of course, the potential global *market* for them is enormous.
7. I've been spending too much recently.	G. Fortunately I receive *unemployment benefit.*
8. In my country, there are a lot of very poor people and only a few rich ones.	H. There is a very uneven *distribution of wealth.*
9. I lost my job last month.	I. The *interest* they pay me is much higher.
10. I retire next month.	J. It's the first time I've *inherited* something.
11. Prices are rising quickly everywhere.	K. It seems to be some kind of tax *rebate.*
12. The January sales start tomorrow.	L. Maybe I should consider getting one *on credit.*

61

For reference, see the *Easier English Dictionary for Students* (0 7475 6624 0)

Money & finance

C. Now read this passage and complete the gaps with one of the words or expressions from Tasks A and B. You may need to change the form of some of the words.

'Financial advice from a father to a son'

In the play 'Hamlet' by William Shakespeare, a father gives his son some financial advice. 'Neither a borrower nor a lender be', he says. He is trying to tell his son that he should never 1_____ money from anyone because it will make it difficult for him to manage his finances. Likewise he should never give a financial 2_____ to a friend because he will probably never see the money again, and will probably lose his friend as well.

The play was written over four hundred years ago, but today many parents would give similar advice to their children. Imagine the conversation they would have now:

Son: Right dad, I'm off to university now.

Father: All right son, but let me give you some sound financial advice before you go.

Son: Oh come on dad.....

Father: Now listen, this is important. The first thing you should do is to make sure you balance your 3_____ - the money you receive from me - and your 4_____ - the money you spend. If you spend too much, you will end up with an 5_____ at the bank. Don't expect me to pay it for you.

Son: But it's so difficult. Things are so expensive, and the 6_____ goes up all the time. 7_____ is running at about 10%.

Father: I know, but you should try to 8_____ . Avoid expensive shops and restaurants. Also, put your money in a good 9_____ . They offer a much higher rate of 10_____ than banks. Also, avoid buying things 11_____ .

Son: Why?

Father: Because shops charge you an 12_____ amount of money to buy things over a period of time. It's much better to 13_____ a little bit of money each week so that when you see something you want, you can buy it outright. Try to wait for the sales, when shops offer huge 14_____ and you can pick up a 15_____ . And try to get a 16_____ .

Son: How do I do that?

Father: Easy. When you buy something, ask the shop if they'll lower the price by, say, 10%. Next, when you eventually get a job and are earning a good salary, try to 17_____ the money in a good company. Buy 18_____ in government organisations or 19_____ in private companies.

Son: OK dad, I've heard enough.

Father: One final piece of advice, son.

Son: What's that dad?

Father: To thine own self be true.

Son: You what?

For reference, see the *Easier English Dictionary for Students* (0 7475 6624 0)

Politics

A. Look at the sentences 1-12 and rearrange the letters in *bold* to make a word connected with politics. (The first and last letters of each word are <u>underlined</u>. A dictionary definition is included to help you.) Then put the words into the grid below. If you do it correctly, you will find a word in the bold vertical strip which means 'rule of a country by one person'.

1. We live in a *me**y**oa**dc**rc. (A country governed by freely elected representatives of the people)*

2. Scotland is aiming for *n**d**npn**i**edc**ee**e in the next few years. (Freedom)*

3. A *a**i**dtd**e**na**c** for the Labour Party called at our house last week. (A person who is standing for election)*

4. The military junta abolished the constitution and set up a *io**a**ialrt**tt**an régime. (Having total power and not allowing any opposition or personal freedom)*

5. An *hu**i**atoitaar**rn** government is not necessarily a bad thing. (Controlling people strictly)*

6. The Prime Minister has appointed a group of *o**c**tthraec**ns** to run the government. (A person with particular skills brought in to run a country or an organisation)*

7. The Conservative Party lost the election and is now in *o**p**sio**n**oti**p**. (The party or group which opposes the government)*

8. France is a *p**i**cub**rel**, with a president and prime minister. (A system of government which is governed by elected representatives headed by an elected or nominated president)*

9. Governments often impose strict economic *on**t**inc**s**as on countries which abuse their power. (Restrictions on trade with a country in order to try to influence its political development)*

10. The American Congress is formed of the *eoHus of Representatives and the Senate. (Part of a parliament)*

11. Her socialist *o**i**ldg**y**oe led her to join the party. (A theory of life based not on religious belief, but on political or economic philosophy)*

12. *liarPatmen has passed a law forbidding the sale of cigarettes to children. (A group of elected representatives who vote the laws of a country)*

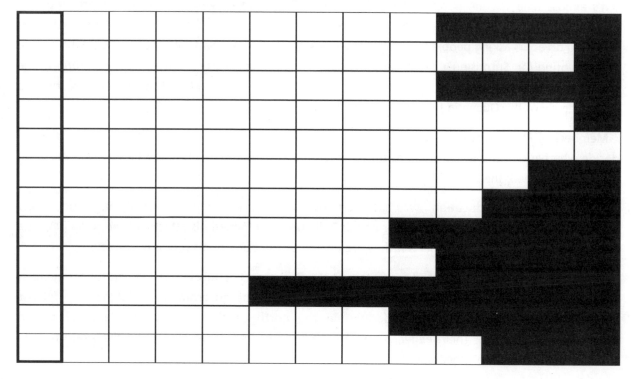

For reference, see the *Easier English Dictionary for Students* (0 7475 6624 0)

Politics

B. Look at these sentences and decide if they are TRUE or FALSE. Use a dictionary to help you.

1. A *monarchy* is a system of government with an elected king or queen.

2. A *politician* is a person who works for the king or queen.

3. A *statesman* or *stateswoman* is an important religious leader or representative of a country.

4. A cabinet is a *committee* formed of the most important members of a government.

5. A *president* is the head of a republic.

6. A *ministry* is a person who works for the government.

7. A *constituency* is an area of a country which elects a Member of Parliament.

8. A *policy* is a government which is controlled by the police.

9. A *referendum* is the process of choosing by voting.

10. An *election* is a vote where all the people of a country are asked to vote on a single question.

C. Now look at this extract from a current affairs radio programme and complete the gaps with one of the words or expressions from Tasks A and B. In some cases, more than one answer may be possible. You may need to change the form of some of the words.

Good evening, and welcome to today's edition of 'Today in Government'

There were angry scenes in both 1_____ of Parliament today following an unprecedented walkout by the Prime Minister and other members of his 2_____ during a speech by the leader of the 3_____ . Criticising their 4_____ on law and order, the Prime Minister called his opposite number a 'strict 5_____ who wants to take away the freedom of the individual and turn the country from a freedom-loving 6_____ to a 7_____ run by one man.'

It's almost time for the people of Britain to vote again and it is now only one month until the 8_____ . All over the country, 9_____ from all the major parties are knocking on doors asking people to vote for them. We conducted a recent survey to find out who people will be voting for. Surprisingly, many support the Workers' Union Party for their policy of turning the country from a 10_____ to a 11_____ : a lot of people support the idea of getting rid of the Queen in favour of an elected president.

Members of Parliament have called for a 12_____ so that the people of Britain can decide whether or not the country joins the 'One Europe' organisation. This follows a survey in the town of Woolhampstead, the Prime Minister's own 13_____ .

The Ministry of Education was accused by the press today of employing too many 14_____ . Chris Smith, editor of the Daily News, defended his attack. 'It's no good having a department full of computer experts if they are unable to run our schools properly', he said.

Michael Yates, a senior statesman for Britain at the European Commission, has called for EU member states to impose strict economic 15_____ on the government of Boland. This follows alleged human rights abuses on tribesmen in the north of the country who are demanding 16_____ . Their leader, Asagai Walumbe, called on countries around the world to help them in their struggle for freedom.

For reference, see the *Easier English Dictionary for Students* (0 7475 6624 0)

The environment

A. Match the first part of each sentence in the left-hand column with its second part in the right-hand column. Use the words in *bold* to help you. Check that each sentence you put together is grammatically correct.

1. Some modern agricultural methods have been heavily criticized,...

2. If you wear a fur coat in public,...

3. It is illegal to kill pandas, tigers...

4. If we don't do more to protect pandas,...

5. A lot of British people are interested in unusual animals,...

6. National parks in Kenya are currently recruiting experts...

7. In an attempt to preserve forests around the country...

8. We would like to carry out more scientific study into rainforests...

9. I don't like zoos because I think...

10. I saw a fascinating documentary about the way animals live in Venezuela and thought...

11. In order to increase the birth rate, the Chinese government has spent a lot of money...

12. Hunters have killed so many animals that...

(A) ...in many countries *poaching* is considered more serious than drug smuggling.

(B) ...and *rare breeds* parks are very popular with many.

(C) ...in *wildlife management.*

(D) ...the government's *conservation programme* has been very successful.

(E) ...they'll soon be *extinct.*

(F) ...with *battery farming* in particular receiving a lot of condemnation.

(G) ...it was fascinating to observe their *natural behaviour.*

(H) ...on a successful panda *breeding* programme.

(I) ...keeping animals in *captivity* is cruel.

(J) ...or any other *endangered species.*

(K) ...but it is often difficult to get people to fund the *research.*

(L) ...you risk coming under attack from *animal rights activists.*

B. Replace the expressions in *bold* with a word or expression from the box which has the same meaning.

| unleaded petrol • fossil fuels • recycle (things) • organic |
| genetically modified • greenhouse • rain forest • global warming |
| erosion • contaminated • environmentalists • emissions |
| biodegradable packaging • acid rain • Green Belt • ecosystem |

1. In Britain, building is restricted or completely banned in the *area of farming land or woods and parks which surrounds a town.*

2. Many companies are developing *boxes, cartons and cans which can easily be decomposed by organisms such as bacteria, or by sunlight, sea, water, etc.*

3. The burning of some fuels creates *carbon dioxide, carbon monoxide, sulphur dioxide, methane and other* gases which rise into the atmosphere.

4. Farmers have cleared hectares of *thick wooded land in tropical regions where the precipitation is very high.*

For reference, see the *Easier English Dictionary for Students* (0 7475 6624 0)

The environment

5. Planting trees provides some protection from the *gradual wearing away* of soil.

6. We should all try to *process waste material so that it can be used again.*

7. These potatoes are *cultivated naturally, without using any chemical fertilisers or pesticides.*

8. This bread is made from wheat which has been *altered at a molecular level so as to change certain characteristics which can be inherited.*

9. More and more cars are built to use *fuel which has been made without lead additives.*

10. *Polluted precipitation which kills trees* falls a long distance away from the source of the pollution.

11. Human beings have had a devastating effect on the *living things, both large and small,* in many parts of the world.

12. The *gases and other substances* which come from factories using oil, coal and other *fuels which are the remains of plants and animals* can cause serious damage to the environment.

13. Don't drink that water! It's been *made dirty by something being added to it.*

14. Friends of the Earth, Greenpeace and other *people concerned with protecting the environment are holding a forum in London next month.*

15. *The heating up of the earth's atmosphere by pollution* is threatening life as we know it.

C. Now look at this essay and complete the gaps with one of the words or expressions from Tasks A and B. In some cases, more than one answer may be possible. You may need to change the form of some of the words.

'Environmental degradation is a major world problem. What causes this problem, and what can we do to prevent it?'

There is no doubt that the environment is in trouble. Factories burn 1_____ which produce 2_____ , and this kills trees. At the same time, 3_____ gases rise into the air and contribute to 4_____ , which threatens to melt the polar ice cap. Meanwhile farmers clear huge areas of 5_____ in places such as the Amazon to produce feeding land for cattle or produce wood for building. Rivers and oceans are so heavily 6_____ by industrial waste that it is no longer safe to go swimming. Cars pump out poisonous 7_____ which we all have to breathe in. 8_____ and overfishing are killing off millions of animals, including whales, elephants and other 9_____ . In fact, all around us, all living things large and small which comprise our finely balanced 10_____ are being systematically destroyed by human greed and thoughtlessness.

There is a lot we can all do, however, to help prevent this. The easiest thing, of course, is to 11_____ waste material such as paper and glass so that we can use it again. We should also check that the things we buy from supermarkets are packaged in 12_____ packaging which decomposes easily. At the same time, we should make a conscious effort to avoid foods which are 13_____ (at least until someone proves that they are safe both for us and for the environment). If you are truly committed to protecting the environment, of course, you should only buy 14_____ fruit and vegetables, safe in the knowledge that they have been naturally cultivated. Finally, of course, we should buy a small car that uses 15_____ which is less harmful to the environment or, even better, make more use of public transport.

The serious 16_____ , however, do much more. They are aware of the global issues involved and will actively involve themselves in 17_____ by making sure our forests are kept safe for future generations. They will oppose activities which are harmful to animals, such as 18_____ . And they will campaign to keep the 19_____ around our towns and cities free from new building.

We cannot all be as committed as them, but we can at least do our own little bit at grass roots level. We, as humans, have inherited the earth, but that doesn't mean we can do whatever we like with it.

For reference, see the *Easier English Dictionary for Students* (0 7475 6624 0)

Healthcare

A. Match the sentence in the left-hand column with a sentence in the right-hand column. Use the words in *bold* to help you.

PROBLEMS

1. Mrs Brady has suffered from terrible *rheumatism* for years.

2. More women than men are affected by *arthritis.*

3. Air conditioning units are often responsible for spreading *infections* around an office.

4. Cardiovascular disease is becoming more common in Britain.

5. Too much exposure to the sun can cause skin *cancer.*

6. It is important not to eat too much food with a high *cholesterol* content.

7. Too many people these days live a *sedentary lifestyle.*

8. People in positions of responsibility often have *stress-related* illnesses.

9. Premature babies are *vulnerable* to illnesses.

10. The National Health Service is suffering from *cutbacks* and *underfunding.*

11. The AIDS *virus* is *incurable.*

(A) Illnesses which affect the *circulation* of blood are particularly common with people who are overweight.

(B) This is deposited on the walls of the *arteries* and can block them.

(C) They can easily be spread from one person to another.

(D) Pains or stiffness in the *joints* or *muscles* can be very difficult to live with.

(E) They don't get enough exercise.

(F) Their *immune system* is not properly developed and can be easily hurt.

(G) The painful *inflammation* of a joint may require *surgery.*

(H) The government has reduced its expenditure in this area.

(I) But there are drugs which can slow down its cell-destroying properties.

(J) Once the body's *cells* start growing abnormally, a cure can be difficult to find.

(K) The pressures of a high-powered job can cause nervous *strain,* which may require drugs.

B. Replace the words or expressions in bold with a word or expression from the box which has the same meaning.

CURES

protein • holistic medicine • a diet • minerals • vitamins therapeutic • traditional medicines • welfare state surgeon • active • consultant • conventional medicine	

1. If you suffer from a bad back, a massage may be *able to cure or relieve the disorder*.

2. One of the secrets of remaining in good health is to choose *food to eat* that is high in fibre and low in fat.

3. Most people, when they are ill, rely on *modern pills and tablets* to cure them.

4. Some *old-fashioned cures for illnesses,* such as herbal tablets and remedies, are becoming increasingly popular.

For reference, see the *Easier English Dictionary for Students* (0 7475 6624 0)

Healthcare

5. Many people are turning to *treatments which involve the whole person, including their mental health, rather than just dealing with the symptoms of the illness.*

6. Doctors sometimes refer their patients to a *medical specialist attached to a hospital.*

7. It takes many years of training to become a *doctor specializing in surgery.*

8. Meat, eggs and nuts are rich sources of *a compound which is an essential part of living cells, and which is essential to keep the human body working properly.*

9. On his holiday, he had to take *essential substances which are not synthesized by the body but are found in food and are needed for growth and health,* because the food he ate lacked the B and C groups.

10. Calcium and zinc are two of the most important *substances found in food.*

11. Most doctors recommend an *energetic* lifestyle, with plenty of exercise.

12. British people enjoy free healthcare thanks to the *large amount of money which is spent to make sure they have adequate health services.*

C. Now look at this extract from a magazine article and complete the gaps with one of the words or expressions from Tasks A and B. In some cases, more than one answer may be possible. You may need to change the form of some of the words.

A cure for the future in the past?

For over fifty years, the people of Britain have relied on the 1_____ to make sure they have adequate health services. But now the National Health Service is sick. Government 2_____ and 3_____ are forcing hospitals to close, and waiting lists for treatment are getting longer. Under such circumstances, it is no surprise that more people are turning to private (but expensive) healthcare.

For some, however, there are alternatives. They are turning their back on modern pills, tablets and other 4_____ . It seems paradoxical, but in an age of microchips and high technology, 5_____ (the old-fashioned cures that our grandparents relied on) is making a comeback. Consider these case studies:

Maude is 76 and has been suffering from 6_____ for almost ten years. "The inflammation in my joints was almost unbearable, and my doctor referred me to a 7_____ at the London Hospital. I was told that I needed 8_____ , but would need to wait for at least two years before I could have the operation. In desperation, I started having massage sessions. To my surprise, these were very 9_____ , and while they didn't cure the disorder, they did relieve it to some extent".

Ron is 46. His high-powered city job was responsible for a series of 10_____ illnesses, and the drugs he took did little to relieve the nervous strain. "I read about treatments which involve the whole person rather than the individual symptoms, but I had always been sceptical about 11_____ . However, my friend recommended a dietician who advised me that part of my problem was 12_____-related. Basically, the foods I was eating were contributing to my disorder. She gave me a list of foods that would provide the right 13_____ and 14_____ to keep me in good health. At the same time, she recommended a more 15_____ lifestyle - running, swimming, that kind of thing. I'm a bit of a couch potato, and the 16_____ lifestyle I had lived was compounding the problem. Now I feel great!"

So is there still a place in our lives for modern medicine? While it is true that some infections and viruses may be prevented by resorting to alternative medicine, more serious illnesses such as 17_____ need more drastic measures. We do need our health service at these times, and we shouldn't stop investing in its future. But we mustn't forget that for some common illnesses, the cure may lie in the past.

For reference, see the *Easier English Dictionary for Students* (0 7475 6624 0)

Travel

A. Look at the following sentences and decide if they are true or false. If they are false, explain why.

1. A *travel agency* is the same as a *tour operator.*

2. A *package tour* is a holiday in which the price includes flights, transfers to and from the airport and accommodation.

3. An *all-inclusive* holiday is a holiday in which the price includes flights, transfers, accommodation, food and drink.

4. When passengers *embark,* they get *off* an aeroplane or ship.

5. When passengers *disembark,* they get *on* an aeroplane or ship.

6. The first thing you do when you go to an airport is go to the *check-in*.

7. The first thing you do when you arrive at your hotel is *check in.*

8. The opposite of a *package tourist* is an *independent traveller.*

9. *Mass tourism* can have a negative effect on the environment.

10. *Eco-tourism* is tourism which has a negative effect on the environment.

11. The words *trip, excursion, journey* and *voyage* all have the same meaning.

12. It is always necessary to have a *visa* when you visit a different country.

13. A flight from London to Paris could be described as a *long-haul* flight.

14. Flying *economy class* is more expensive than flying *business class*.

15. A Canadian citizen flying to Japan will have to fill in an *immigration card* before he arrives.

B. Complete sentences 1-11 with a suitable word or expression from the box.

deported	• expatriates	•	internally displaced
repatriated	• immigration	• UNHCR •	persona non grata
economic migrants	• culture shock	• emigration •	refugees

1. At the beginning of the war, thousands of _____ fled over the border to the next country.

2. Since the civil war began, almost a million people have been forced to move to another part of the country. These _____ persons are now without food or shelter.

3. Nineteenth-century governments encouraged _____ to the colonies.

4. The government is encouraging _____ because of the shortage of workers in key industries.

5. Going from California to live with hill tribes in India was something of a _____ .

6. Thousands of British _____ live in Singapore, where many of them have high-powered jobs.

7. The _____ is under a lot of pressure owing to the huge number of displaced persons around the world.

8. He was _____ from the country when his visa expired.

9. Because he had a criminal record, the government didn't want him to enter the country, declared him _____ and asked him to leave immediately.

10. After the economy collapsed in the east, thousands of _____ headed west in the hope of finding a good job.

11. He didn't want to be _____ , but nevertheless was put on a plane back home.

For reference, see the *Easier English Dictionary for Students* (0 7475 6624 0)

Travel

C. Now look at this essay and complete the gaps with one of the words or expressions from Tasks A and B. In some cases, more than one answer may be possible. You may need to change the form of some of the words.

Travel: the other side of the coin

Most of us have, at some point in our lives, experienced the joys of travel. We go to the 1_____ to pick up our brochures. We book a two-week 2_____ with flights and accommodation included (or if we are 3_____ , we make our own way to the country and travel around from place to place with a rucksack on our back). We make sure we have all the right currency, our passport and any 4_____ that are necessary to get us into the country. We go to the airport and 5_____ . We strap ourselves into our tiny 6_____ aircraft seats and a few hours later we 7_____ from the aircraft, strange new sights, smells and sounds greeting us. Nowadays, it seems, the whole world goes on holiday at once: the age of 8_____ is in full swing!

But for the great majority of people around the world, travel for them is done in the face of great adversity and hardship. They never get to indulge in an 9_____ holiday in a luxury hotel with all meals and drinks included. They never get to explore the lush Amazon rain forest or the frozen wastes of the Arctic on an 10_____ holiday. For them, travel is a matter of life and death. I refer, of course, to all the 11_____ escaping from their own countries, or the 12_____ , moved from one part of their country to another by an uncaring government, or 13_____ forced to find a job and seek a living wherever they can.

Can you imagine anything worse than the misery these people must face? Let's not confuse them with those 14_____ , who choose to live in another country and often have nice houses and high salaries. These people are simply desperate to survive. As well as losing their homes because of war or famine or other natural disasters, they must come to terms with their new environment: for many, the 15_____ can be too great. And while many countries with an open policy on 16_____ will welcome them in with open arms, others will simply turn them away. These people become 17_____ , unwanted and unwelcome. Even if they manage to get into a country, they will often be 18_____ or repatriated. Their future is uncertain.

Something to think about, perhaps, the next time you are 19_____ to your five-star hotel by a palm-fringed beach or sitting in a coach on an 20_____ to a pretty castle in the countryside.

> *Don't forget to keep a record of the words and expressions that you have learnt, review your notes from time to time and try to use new vocabulary items whenever possible.*

For reference, see the *Easier English Dictionary for Students* (0 7475 6624 0)

Crime & the law

A. Match the words and expressions in the box with their correct definition 1-9.

law-abiding •	solicitor •	defendant •	jury
offender •	victim •	barrister •	judge • witness

1. A person appointed to make legal decisions in a court of law.

2. A group of twelve citizens who are sworn to decide whether someone is guilty or innocent on the basis of evidence given in a court of law.

3. A person who sees something happen or is present when something happens.

4. A person who is accused of doing something illegal.

5. A person who is attacked or who is in an accident.

6. A qualified lawyer who gives advice to members of the public and acts for them in legal matters.

7. A person who commits an offence against the law.

8. A lawyer who can present a case in court.

9. An expression used to describe someone who obeys the law.

B. The following groups of sentences describe the legal process which follows a crime. However, with the exception of the first sentence, the sentences in each group are in the wrong order. Put them into the correct order, using the key words in bold to help you. Some of these words appear in Task A.

Part 1

A. One night, Jim Smith **committed** a serious crime. = *Sentence 1*

B. Jim asked the officer for a **solicitor** to help him.

C. At the same time, the police arranged for a **barrister** to **prosecute** him.

D. They took him to the police station and formally **charged** him with the crime.

E. When the **trial** began and he appeared in **court** for the first time, he **pleaded** his **innocence.**

F. The next morning the police **arrested** him.

Part 2

A. His barrister also said he was **innocent** and asked the court to **acquit** him. = *Sentence 1*

B. While he was in prison, he applied for **parole.**

C. As a result, the judge **sentenced** him to two years in prison.

D. He was **released** after 18 months.

E. However, there were several **witnesses,** and the **evidence** against him was overwhelming.

F. Having all the **proof** they needed, the **jury** returned a **guilty verdict.**

> *Don't forget to keep a record of the words and expressions that you have learnt, review your notes from time to time and try to use new vocabulary items whenever possible.*

For reference, see the *Easier English Dictionary for Students* (0 7475 6624 0)

Crime & the law

Part 3

A. Unfortunately, prison failed to *rehabilitate* him and after his *release* he continued with his *misdeeds,* attacking an old woman in the street. = *Sentence 1*

B. Jim promised to *reform* and the pensioner withdrew her call for more severe *retribution.*

C. With this in mind, instead of passing a *custodial sentence,* he *fined* him a lot of money and ordered him to do *community service.*

D. He was *re-arrested* and returned to court.

E. His new *victim,* a pensioner, thought that the judge was being too *lenient* on Jim and called for the reinstatement of *corporal punishment* and *capital punishment!*

F. At his second trial the judge agreed that prison was not a *deterrent* for Jim.

C. Now look at this extract from a politician's speech and complete the gaps with one of the words or expressions from Tasks A and B. In some cases, more than one answer may be possible. You may need to change the form of some of the words.

Are you worried about crime? I am. We read it every day in the papers. A terrible crime has been 1_____ , the police have 2_____ someone, he has appeared in front of a jury in 3_____ , he has 4_____ his innocence but has been found 5_____ of his crime and he has been 6_____ to ten years in prison. We are all very relieved that the criminal is being punished for his 7_____ , and 8_____ citizens like you and me can sleep more safely at night.

But what happens next? We all hope, don't we, that the prisoner will benefit from society's 9_____ , that a spell in prison will 10_____ him and make him a better person. We all hope that he will 11_____ and become like us. We all hope that when he is eventually 12_____ and let loose on the streets, he will be a good character, the threat of another spell in jail being a suitable 13_____ which will stop him from breaking the law again. Oh yes.

But let's face it. The reality is usually very different. The prisoner may be released on 14_____ , before the end of his sentence. He will try to re-enter society. But then he often becomes a 15_____ himself, unable to find work and rejected by society. It isn't long before he's back in prison again.

So what alternatives are there, I hear you say. What can we do to the 16_____ to make sure he doesn't commit another crime? There are alternatives to prison, of course, such as 17_____ in which he will provide a service to those around him. Or he can pay a large 18_____ . Alternatively, we could establish a more severe system of punishment, including 19_____ and 20_____ , but we like to consider ourselves civilised, and the idea of beating or executing someone is repellent to us. Oh yes.

The answer, of course, is far simpler. We need to be tough not on the criminal, but on the cause of the crime. We should spend less of the taxpayer's money funding the 21_____ and 22_____ and all the other people who work for the legal system, and put the money instead into supporting deprived areas which are the breeding grounds for crime. We in the ConLab Party believe that everybody needs a good chance in life, and this is a good step forward. Vote for us now!

Don't forget to keep a record of the words and expressions that you have learnt, review your notes from time to time and try to use new vocabulary items whenever possible.

For reference, see the *Easier English Dictionary for Students* (0 7475 6624 0)

Social tensions

A. Match each newspaper headline in the box with the first line of its accompanying story below. Use the underlined words and expressions to help you.

A. *ILLEGAL ALIENS* TO BE EXPELLED

B. *ETHNIC MINORITIES* 'LIVING BELOW *POVERTY* LEVEL'

C. *HOMELESS SQUATTERS* EVICTED

D. *INSTITUTIONAL RACISM* STILL A PROBLEM

E. *INTERNALLY DISPLACED* IN NEW *GENOCIDE* HORROR

F. *EXTREMISTS* ACCUSED OF INCITING *RACIAL HATRED*

G. *UNREST, RIOTS* AND *ANARCHY* CONTINUE

H. *REBELS* VICTORIOUS IN LATEST *POWER STRUGGLE*

I. *DISCRIMINATION* AND *EXPLOITATION* A MAJOR PROBLEM IN BRITISH INDUSTRY

J. *DISSIDENTS* ASK AUSTRALIAN GOVERNMENT FOR *POLITICAL ASYLUM*

---

1. Officers from the Thames Valley Police Force raided a house in Kidlington earlier this morning and forcibly removed a family who had been staying there illegally since they lost their home in August.

2. Almost 50% of factory workers in national companies claim they have received bad treatment or have been taken advantage of because of their class, religion, race , language, colour or sex, it has been revealed.

3. The UN has accused the government of Zarislavia of further atrocities committed in the west of the country, where hundreds of migrants are reported to have been killed by security forces.

4. Opponents of the government in Yugaria have asked to stay in Sydney because the political situation in their own country is making it unsafe for them to return.

5. The police have once again been accused of discriminating against minority groups, despite their reassurances earlier this year that they had reformed their practices.

6. Neo-Nazi groups in Paris were today condemned for inciting violence against non-whites in the centre of the city.

7. A shocking survey has revealed that almost 30% of Asian and African racial groups living in London are suffering financial hardship.

8. Following further devaluation of the Malovian dollar, violence has once again erupted on the streets of the capital.

9. Groups fighting against the government of George Malikes in Livatia have succeeded in capturing and occupying the parliament building.

10. The Government has ordered the immediate deportation of over 200 immigrants who entered the country without passports or visas last year.

73

For reference, see the *Easier English Dictionary for Students* (0 7475 6624 0)

Social tensions

B. Match the words and expressions in the first box with a word or expression in the second box which is either the closest in meaning or which is normally associated with it. Some of these also appear in Task A.

| ethnic cleansing • prejudice • civil rights • harassment |
| rebel • picket line • poverty-stricken • refugee • outcast |

| reject (noun) • non-conformist • blackleg • human rights • destitute |
| discrimination • displaced person • intimidation • racial purging |

C. Now look at this news programme and complete the gaps with one of the words or expressions from Tasks A and B. In some cases, more than one answer may be possible. You may need to change the form of some of the words.

Good evening. Here is the news.

Neo-Nazis and other 1_____ have been held responsible for a wave of 2_____ in the Bratilovan Republic. The United Nations estimates that over 20,000 people have been murdered there in the last six months. 3_____ who have escaped from the country have asked the British government to grant them 4_____ , as they fear for their safety if they have to return.

The government are to deport 500 5_____ whose visas have expired. Angry members of the opposition have accused the government of 6_____ , as most of the deportees are of African origin. Meanwhile, the police have been accused of 7_____ , after Asian families in Bradford complained they had been pestered and worried by officers following a series of robberies in the city.

8_____ leaders in the USA have held a demonstration in Washington against the death penalty. They have called for a total abolition of capital punishment, claiming that it is contrary to basic 9_____ principles outlined in the United Nations Declaration of Human Rights.

10_____ fighting the government of President Stanislow have taken control of the television station in the centre of the capital. This follows a long-standing 11_____ . between Mr Stanislow and the principal opposition party which has seriously weakened his power.

A spokesman for the 12_____ community in London has presented a petition to the government asking them to provide housing for everyone. He argues that the government's refusal to raise the minimum wage rate has resulted in thousands living in 13_____ , with not enough money to pay for somewhere to live. Meanwhile, the Metropolitan Police evicted several 14_____ who took over a house in the city centre last week and refused to leave until the government took positive action.

A recent survey reveals that at least 30% of public companies have been accused of 15_____ and 16_____ in the past year. The main offender is Anglo-Amalgamated Telecommunications, a Bristol-based company. Their employees, many of them Asian women, claim they have received bad treatment or been taken advantage of by the company.

And finally, the Cardiff police are preparing for angry scenes at the Welsh International Computers factory tomorrow when 17_____ , anxious to return to work after six months on strike, will attempt to break through the picket line. A senior officer has expressed his concern that there will be 18_____ and people will get hurt as a result.

For reference, see the *Easier English Dictionary for Students* (0 7475 6624 0)

Science & technology

A. Replace the words and expressions in bold in sentences 1 - 18 with a word or expression from the box.

```
analysed  •  genetic engineering  •  breakthrough  •  molecular biology
a technophobe  •  safeguards  •  development  •  cybernetics  •  invented
nuclear engineering  •  combined  •  life expectancy  •  discovered
a technophile  •  innovations  •  react  •  an experiment  •  research
```

1. The company is carrying out **scientific study** to find a cure for Aids.

2. The **planning and production** of the new computer system will take some time.

3. Modern home entertainment systems and other **modern inventions** are changing everyone's lives.

4. Some elements **change their chemical composition** when mixed with water.

5. The scientists have **created** a new machine to automate the process.

6. Who was the person who **found** penicillin?

7. When the food was **examined closely and scientifically,** it was found to contain bacteria.

8. Rain **joined together** with CO_2 gases produces acid rain.

9. Ron is **terrified of modern technology.**

10. Geoff is **very interested in modern technology.**

11. **Protection** against accidents in this laboratory are minimal.

12. Scientists conducted **a scientific test** to see how people react to different smells.

13. Brian is studying **the techniques used to change the genetic composition of a cell so as to change certain characteristics which can be inherited.**

14. Sarah is studying **the things which form the structure of living matter.**

15. Christine is studying **how information is communicated in machines and electronic devices in comparison with how it is communicated in the brain and nervous system.**

16. Neil is studying **the different ways of extracting and controlling energy from atomic particles.**

17. There has been a **sudden success** in the search for a cure for cancer.

18. **The number of years a person is likely to live** has increased a great deal thanks to modern medicine and technology.

For reference, see the *Easier English Dictionary for Students* (0 7475 6624 0)

Science & technology

B. Read this description of a computer. Unfortunately, the person who is describing it is not very familiar with computer terminology and cannot remember all the words. Help them by using the appropriate word or expression in the box to give a more scientific definition of their words in bold.

log on • keyboard • load / install • virus • e-mail • download
hardware • crashed • software • Internet • scanner • mouse
base unit / disk drive • website • printer • monitor

OK, here's my new computer. As you can see, there are five main parts. Now, the **large box with the slots and sliding disk carrier** (1) _____ is the most important part. It carries all the **stuff that makes the computer work** (2)_____. You can also **put in** (3)_____ your own games and other **things** (4)_____. Next to it there is the **thing that looks like a small television** (5)_____ so that you can see what the computer is doing. To the right of that, there is the **machine that lets you make black and white or colour copies of the documents that you create on the computer** (6)_____. You can control the computer by using the **rectangular flat thing with all the letters and numbers on** (7)_____ or the **funny little object with the long lead which you can move across your desk** (8)_____. The large flat thing to the left of the computer is the **machine you can use to make copies of your photographs onto the computer, a bit like a photocopier** (9)_____.

It's a very useful machine, of course. Once you **get it up and running** (10)_____ you can do lots of things on it. You can create documents, play games or get information from the **fantastic thing that links computers from around the world** (11)_____. A lot of companies and organizations have their own **special computer page** (12)_____ which you can look at, and you can **transfer** (13)_____ the information to your own computer files. Or, if you like, you can send messages to other people by using **a special electronic letter-sending facility** (14)_____.

Unfortunately, I can't let you use it as it **stopped working** (15)_____ last night. It's probably got a **technical fault, usually created on purpose, that affects computer files and folders** (16)_____.

Don't forget to keep a record of the words and expressions that you have learnt, review your notes from time to time and try to use new vocabulary items whenever possible.

For reference, see the *Easier English Dictionary for Students* (0 7475 6624 0)

Science & technology

C. Now look at this essay and fill in the gaps with one of the words or expressions from Tasks A and B. In some cases, more than one answer may be possible. You may need to change some of the word forms.

Technology has come a long way in the last fifty years, and our lives have become better as a result. Or have they?

The second half of the twentieth century saw more changes than in the previous two hundred years. Penicillin has already been 1_____ and used to treat infections; there have been many remarkable advances in medicine that have helped to increase our average 2_____ way beyond that of our ancestors. Incredible 3_____ such as television have changed the way we spend our leisure hours. Perhaps the most important 4_____ , however, has been the microchip. Nobody could have imagined, when it was first 5_____ , that within a matter of years, this tiny piece of silicon and circuitry would be found in almost every household object from the kettle to the video recorder. And nobody could have predicted the sudden proliferation of computers that would completely change our lives, allowing us to access information from the other side of the world via the 6_____ or send messages around the world by 7_____ at the touch of a button. Meanwhile, 8_____ into other aspects of information technology is making it easier and cheaper for us to talk to friends and relations around the world. Good news for 9_____ who love modern technology, bad news for the 10_____ who would prefer to hide from these modern miracles.

But everything has a price. The development of 11_____ led to mass automation in factories, which in turn led to millions losing their jobs. The genius of Einstein led to the horrors of the atomic bomb and the dangerous uncertainties of 12_____ (we hear of accidents and mishaps at nuclear power stations around the world, where 13_____ to prevent accidents were inadequate). The relatively new science of 14_____ has been seen as a major step forward, but putting modified foods onto the market before scientists had properly 15_____ them was perhaps one of the most irresponsible decisions of the 1990s. Meanwhile, pharmaceutical companies continue to 16_____ on animals, a move that many consider to be cruel and unnecessary.

Of course we all rely on modern science and technology to improve our lives. However, we need to make sure that we can control it before it controls us.

> *Don't forget to keep a record of the words and expressions that you have learnt, review your notes from time to time and try to use new vocabulary items whenever possible.*

For reference, see the *Easier English Dictionary for Students* (0 7475 6624 0)

Food & diet

A. Find words in the box below which have the same meaning as the dictionary definitions 1-11. A sample sentence with the word removed has been given to you.

1. Units of measurement of energy in food.

    (Example: She's counting _____ to try and lose weight)

2. A compound which is an essential part of living cells, one of the elements in food which you need to keep the human body working properly.

    (Example: Eggs are a rich source of _____)

3. A chemical substance containing carbon, hydrogen and oxygen.

    (Example: Bread, potatoes and rice are good sources of _____)

4. A white substance from plants or animals which can be used for cooking.

    (Example: Fry the meat and drain off the _____)

5. Matter in food which cannot be digested and passes out of the body.

    (Example: A diet that doesn't contain enough _____ can cause intestinal problems)

6. A fatty substance found in fats and oils, also produced by the liver and forming an essential part of all cells.

    (Example: If you eat too much _____ , it can be deposited on the walls of arteries, causing them to become blocked)

7. Essential substance which is not synthesised by the body but is found in food and is needed for health and growth.

    (Example: He doesn't eat enough fruit and suffers from _____ C deficiency)

8. Substance which is found in food, but which can also be dug out of the earth.

    (Example: What is the _____ content of spinach?)

9. Too heavy, often as a result of eating too much.

    (Example: The doctor says I'm _____ and must go on a diet)

10. The result of not having enough to eat, or the result of eating too much of the wrong sort of food.

    (Example: Many of the children in the refugee camp were _____)

11. Receiving food.

    (Example: We are developing a scheme to improve _____ in the poorer areas)

W	E	C	R	T	Y	U	H	F	V	F	H	E	N
M	C	A	R	B	O	H	Y	D	R	A	T	E	S
Y	S	L	C	E	A	C	Z	Q	W	T	E	R	T
U	I	O	H	E	R	V	Z	X	C	V	B	N	M
A	P	R	O	T	E	I	N	A	D	F	G	H	J
K	L	I	L	N	U	T	R	I	T	I	O	N	M
C	V	E	E	B	N	A	Z	X	C	V	B	N	M
L	K	S	S	J	H	M	I	N	E	R	A	L	B
M	N	B	T	V	C	I	L	K	J	H	G	F	D
U	Y	T	E	W	E	N	R	T	Y	U	I	O	P
F	I	B	R	E	A	E	Q	W	E	D	G	T	X
H	E	D	O	V	E	R	W	E	I	G	H	T	B
C	M	A	L	N	O	U	R	I	S	H	E	D	Y
Q	W	E	G	S	T	C	V	T	W	R	D	W	T

For reference, see the *Easier English Dictionary for Students* (0 7475 6624 0)

Food & diet

B. Match sentences 1-10 with a second sentence A-J. Use the key words in *bold* to help you.

1. A lot of people are *allergic* to nuts.
2. Many people do not trust *genetically modified* foods.
3. *Organic* vegetables are more expensive but are better for you.
4. We refuse to eat *battery chickens*.
5. We prefer to eat *free range* meats.
6. The *harvest* has been very bad this year.
7. Following the floods in Mozambique, there was a terrible *scarcity* of food.
8. There has been an outbreak of *salmonella, listeria* and other *food poisoning* in Perth.
9. Too many people don't eat a *balanced diet.*
10. *Fast food* is very popular.

A. This is because they are cultivated naturally, without using any chemical fertilisers or pesticides.
B. There wasn't enough to feed everyone affected by the disaster.
C. They are not sure that altering the composition of cells to change certain characteristics is safe.
D. It's good to know that the animals were given enough space to express their natural behaviour.
E. Terrible weather conditions have prevented the crops from ripening and reduced the yield.
F. A lot of people are in hospital as a result.
G. Unfortunately, a diet of burgers, pizzas and fried chicken is not very healthy.
H. They physically react very badly.
I. This is because they spend their life confined in a small cage.
J. They don't consume sufficient quantities of the different food groups.

C. Now complete this article with one of the words or expressions from Tasks A and B. In some cases, more than one answer may be possible. You may need to change some of the word forms.

Most children enjoy eating 1_____ , but scientific tests have shown us that burgers and pizzas can lack essential 2_____ and 3_____ which are essential for health and growth, while simultaneously containing large amounts of 4_____ and 5_____ which can result in obesity and heart problems. Many children end up suffering from 6_____ , since they eat too much of the wrong sort of food. In fact, in many areas of the developed world, a lot of children show similar symptoms to those in poorer developing countries, where 7_____ of food causes thousands of deaths from starvation, especially in the wake of natural disasters which ruin crops and in some cases totally destroy the annual 8_____ .

Dieticians tell us that we must eat a 9_____ , as it is essential we consume sufficient quantities of the different food groups. They tell us that we should all eat more 10_____, which cannot be digested by the body, and fewer foods which are high in 11_____ , as this can block the walls of arteries and lead to heart problems. This is good advice, of course, but our lifestyles often make this difficult. Many of the ready-prepared foods we buy from supermarkets are high in 12_____ , giving us more energy than we actually need. 13_____ foods are appearing on our supermarket shelves, even though nobody is really sure if altering the composition of food cells is safe. We have the option, of course, of buying 14_____ foods, but naturally-cultivated fruits and vegetables are expensive. And to make matters worse, we are continually hearing about outbreaks of 15_____ and 16_____ which put us off eating certain foods, as nobody wants to spend time in hospital suffering from 17_____ .

A few things to watch out for next time you go shopping. If you have the time and the money, that is!

79

Children & the family

A. Complete these sentences with an appropriate word or expression from A, B or C.

1. Mr and Mrs Smith live at home with their two children. They are a typical example of a modern _____ family
   A. extended   *B. nuclear*   *C. compact*

2. Mr and Mrs Popatlal live at home with their aged parents, children and grandchildren. They are a typical example of a traditional _____ family
   A. nuclear   *B. enlarged*   *C. extended*

3. Mrs Jones lives on her own and has to look after her two children. There are a lot of _____ families like hers
   A. single-parent   *B. mother-only*   *C. mono-parent*

4. Some parents need to _____ their children more strictly
   A. bring down   *B. bring about*   *C. bring up*

5. When I was a child, I had a very turbulent _____
   A. upbringing   *B. upraising*   *C. uplifting*

6. Mrs Kelly is _____ and finds it difficult to look after her children on her own
   A. divorced   *B. divided*   *C. diverged*

7. Many men believe that _____ is the responsibility of a woman
   A. childhelp   *B. childcare*   *C. childaid*

8. _____ is a particularly difficult time of life for a child
   A. convalescence   *B. adolescence*   *C. convergence*

9. A person's behaviour can sometimes be traced back to his/her _____
   A. creative years   *B. formulating years* *C. formative years*

10. The country has seen a sharp drop in the _____ in the last few years
    A. birth rate   *B. baby rate*   *C. born rate*

11. She has five _____ who rely on her to look after them
    A. dependants   *B. dependers*   *C. dependents*

12. _____ is on the rise, with over 20% of serious crimes being committed by children under the age of seventeen
    A. junior crime   *B. juvenile delinquency*   *C. minor crime*

B. Match sentences 1-12 with a second sentence A-M. Use the key words and expressions in bold to help you.

1. Mr and Mrs White are very **authoritarian** parents.

2. Mr. Bowles is considered to be too **lenient**.

3. Mr and Mrs Harris lead **separate lives**.

4. Billy is a **well-adjusted** kid.

5. The Mannings are not very **responsible** parents.

6. My parents are **separated**.

7. Parents must look after their children, but they shouldn't be **over-protective**.

8. Professor Maynard has made a study of the **cognitive processes** of young children.

9. I'm afraid my youngest child is **running wild**.

80

10. She looks quite different from all her **siblings**.

11. There are several **different and distinct stages of development** in a child's life.

12. Tony was raised by a **foster family** when his own parents died.

A. They don't look after their children very well.

B. He is fascinated by the way they learn new things.

C. He very rarely punishes his children.

D. I live with my mother and visit my father at weekends.

E. He never listens to a word I say, and is always playing truant from school.

F. Brothers and sisters usually bear some resemblance to one another.

G. Although they are married and live together, they rarely speak to each other.

H. They are very strict with their children.

I. Of all of these, the teenage years are the most difficult.

J. Children need the freedom to get out and experience the world around them.

K. He's happy at home and is doing well at school.

L. My families take in children who are not their own.

C. Now read this case study and fill in the gaps with one of the words or expressions from Tasks A and B. In some cases, more than one answer may be possible. You may need to change some of the word forms.

Bob's problems began during his 1_____ years. His parents got 2_____ when he was young, and neither of them wanted to raise him or his brother and sister, so he was 3_____ by a 4_____ chosen by his parents' social worker. Unfortunately, his foster-father was a strict 5_____ and often beat him. Bob rebelled against this strict 6_____ , and by the time he was eight, he was already 7_____ , stealing from shops and playing truant. By the time he reached 8_____ , sometime around his thirteenth birthday, he had already appeared in court several times, charged with 9_____ . The judge blamed his foster parents, explaining that children needed 10_____ parents and guardians who would look after them properly. The foster father objected to this, pointing out that Bob's 11_____ - his two brothers and sister - were 12_____ children who behaved at home and worked well at school.

This has raised some interesting questions about the modern family system. While it is true that parents should not be too 13_____ with children by letting them do what they want when they want, or be too 14_____ by sheltering them from the realities of life, it is also true that they should not be too strict. It has also highlighted the disadvantages of the modern 15_____ family where the child has only its mother and father to rely on (or the 16_____ family, in which the mother or father has to struggle particularly hard to support their 17_____). In fact, many believe that we should return to traditional family values and the 18_____ family: extensive research has shown that children from these families are generally better behaved and have a better chance of success in later life.

For reference, see the *Easier English Dictionary for Students* (0 7475 6624 0)

On the road

A. Choose the most suitable explanation or interpretation, A or B, for the following sentences. Use the words in _bold_ to help you.

1. People enjoy the **mobility** that owning a car gives them.
    A. *People enjoy being able to travel easily from one place to another.*
    B. *People enjoy being able to drive very fast.*

2. What's your **destination**?
    A. *Where have you come from?*
    B. *Where are you going to?*

3. **Congestion** in the city centre has increased dramatically.
    A. *It is now easier to drive around the city centre than it was before.*
    B. *It is now more difficult to drive around the city centre than it was before.*

4. The local council wants to reduce the risks to **pedestrians.**
    A. *The local council wants to make it safer for people to walk along the street.*
    B. *The local council wants to make it safer for drivers and their passengers.*

5. Lead-free petrol reduces the risk of **pollution**.
    A. *Lead-free petrol does not make the environment as dirty as conventional petrol.*
    B. *Cars fuelled by lead-free pollution are safer to drive.*

6. **Traffic-calming** measures are becoming increasingly common throughout the country.
    A. *People have to drive more slowly because of the increased number of police in villages and towns.*
    B. *People have to drive more carefully through towns and villages because of specially-built obstacles in the road.*

7. The centre of Camford has been designated a **traffic-free zone.**
    A. *You cannot take your car into the centre of Camford.*
    B. *You can park your car for free in the centre of Camford.*

8. Container lorries and other large vehicles **dominate** our roads.
    A. *There are a lot of large vehicles on the roads.*
    B. *There aren't many large vehicles on the roads.*

9. Young drivers have a higher **accident risk** than older drivers.
    A. *Young drivers are more likely than older drivers to be involved in a crash.*
    B. *Young drivers are less likely than older drivers to be involved in a crash.*

10. Public transport is heavily **subsidised** in most areas.
    A. *The government has made public transport cheaper to use by giving money to bus and train companies.*
    B. *The government has made public transport more expensive to use by increasing the price of road tax.*

11. The junction of London Road and Holly Street is an accident **black spot.**
    A. *A lot of traffic accidents happen here.*
    B. *Not many accidents happen here.*

12. The city council needs to adopt an effective **transport strategy** within the next five years.
    A. *The city council needs to find a better way for people to get into, around and out of the city.*
    B. *The city council needs to encourage more drivers to bring their cars into the city.*

For reference, see the *Easier English Dictionary for Students* (0 7475 6624 0)

B. Look at sentences 1-10 and decide what has, or hasn't, happened (sentences A-J). Use the words in bold to help you.

1. Ambulance driver to policeman: 'The *pedestrian's injuries* are very severe and he has to go to hospital.'
2. Judge to driver: '*Drink-driving* is a serious offence and I therefore ban you from driving for a year'.
3. Driving instructor to student driver: 'Stop! That's a *pedestrian crossing*!'
4. Examiner to student driver: 'You don't know enough about *the Highway Code* yet to pass your theory test.'
5. Policeman to driver: 'Do you realise you were *speeding* back there, sir?'
6. Driver to a friend: 'I can't believe it! He gave me a heavy *fine* and six points on my licence.'
7. Police officer to radio interviewer: '*Joyriding* has increased by almost 50% and I am urging everyone to think twice before they get involved in this stupid activity.'
8. Television news presenter: 'So far this year there have been 27 *fatalities* on Oxfordshire's roads.'
9. City council officer to journalist: 'As part of our new transport strategy, we are going to construct *cycle lanes* in and around the city.'
10. City council officer to journalist: 'The *"Park and Ride"* scheme has been very successful over the last year'.

A. Somebody is unfamiliar with the government publication containing the rules for people travelling on roads.
B. More people have been leaving their cars in designated areas outside a city and catching a bus into the city centre.
C. A lot of cars have been stolen, mainly by young people who want some excitement.
D. A person walking in the street has been hit and badly hurt by a vehicle.
E. Somebody has decided to make it safer to use bicycles.
F. Somebody has almost driven through a red light and hit a person walking across the road.
G. Somebody has had to pay money because of a driving offence.
H. Somebody has consumed an illegal amount of alcohol before driving their car.
I. A lot of people have been killed in traffic-related accidents.
J. Somebody has been driving too fast.

C. Now read this article and fill in the gaps with one of the words or expressions from Tasks A and B. In some cases, more than one answer may be possible. You may need to change some of the word forms.

1_____ and 2_____ on Britain's roads are increasing from year to year: last year, 2,827 people were killed and almost 300,000 hurt in traffic-related accidents. Most of these were caused by drivers 3_____ in built-up areas, where many seem to disregard the 30mph limit, or 4_____ , especially around Christmas, when more alcohol is consumed than at any other time. In many cases, it is 5_____ who are the victims, knocked down as they are walking across the street at 6_____ by drivers who seem to have forgotten that the rules of the 7_____ order you to stop at red lights.

But these innocent victims, together with the help of the police and local councils, are fighting back. In Oxford, a city plagued by 8_____ and 9_____ caused by traffic, and a notorious accident 10_____ for pedestrians and cyclists, the city council has recently implemented its new 11_____ , which has improved the flow of traffic to the benefit of those on foot or on two wheels. 12_____ measures such as bollards and speed humps have slowed traffic down. 13_____ schemes have helped reduce the number of cars in the city, as office workers and shoppers leave their cars outside the city and bus in instead. Cornmarket Street, the main shopping thoroughfare, has been designated a 14_____ , closed to all vehicles during the day. There are more 15_____ on main routes into the city, making it safer for the huge number of students and residents who rely on bicycles to get around. And 16_____ public transport has helped to keep down the cost of using buses. Meanwhile, the police and the courts are coming down hard on drivers who misuse the roads, handing down large 17_____ on selfish, inconsiderate drivers who believe it is their right to 18_____ the roads.

For reference, see the *Easier English Dictionary for Students* (0 7475 6624 0)

The arts

A. Look at sentences 1-10, which are all extracts from art reviews, and decide what is being talked about in each one. Choose the most appropriate answer from the box. There are some which are not needed.

Performing arts

a modern dance piece • a concert • a play • an opera • a film • a ballet

Literature

poetry • a biography • drama • a novel • a collection of short stories

Fine / Visual Arts

abstract art • a landscape • photography • a portrait • a still life • a sculpture

---

1. Mimi Latouche is getting a little too old for this kind of thing, and as I watched her pirouette across the stage in a tutu two sizes too small, she reminded me not so much of a swan as a rather ungainly crow.

2. The scenery was wonderful. The costumes were marvellous. The cast were incredible. I wish I could say the same about the script. The playwright should be shot.

3. In his new book on Ernest Hemingway, acclaimed writer Michael Norris has brought the great man to life in a way nobody else could.

4. Move over Michelangelo! You have a rival. Vittorio Manelleto's marble pieces embody the human form in a way that has not been achieved in over five hundred years.

5. I had to study the picture for almost two minutes before I realised who it was. It was none other than our Queen. I doubt she would have been amused.

6. There are no great tenors in Britain. That is until now. Brian Clack's performance in La Traviatta sent shudders down my spine. What a man! What a voice! What a size!

7. Herbert von Caravan has been conducting now for almost forty years, and his final appearance yesterday was greeted with remarkable applause from both musicians and members of the audience.

8. 'Stone Angel' is an hilarious tale about the fall and rise of an opera singer. I picked it up and didn't put it down until I had finished. A fantastic book.

9. Dylan Thomas showed remarkable eloquence, and this latest compilation of some of his finest prose will surely be a bestseller.

10. Bruschetta's studies of dead animals might not be to everyone's taste, but it is impossible to deny his skill in representing inanimate objects like these on canvas.

11. He usually works in black and white, and in my opinion that's the medium he should stick to. His colour shots are too static and are heavily over-filtered, the strong lighting washes out any subtlety, and much of it is out of focus.

12. Shot entirely on location in Iran, this is perhaps the director's finest hour. A stunning setting, fine performances from the leads, and a cast of thousands of extras make this a truly visual feast.

B. Complete these sentences with an appropriate word or expression from *A, B* or *C*.

1. Tonight's _____ of 'Hamlet' begins at 7.30.
   A. perform   *B. performing*   *C. performance*

2. Camford University Press have just released a collection of Shakespeare's _____ .
   A. works   *B. workers*   *C. workings*

3. The rock group 'Glass Weasel' have released a limited _____ of their new album which contains a CD-Rom of their latest show.
   A. edit   *B. edition*   *C. editor*

4. His last book received excellent _____ in the newspapers.
   A. reviews   *B. previews*   *C. revisions*

5. There is an _____ of Monet's work at the Tate.
   A. exhibitionist   *B. exhibit*   *C. exhibition*

6. The British National Orchestra is delighted with the government's promise of a £500,000 _____ .
   A. subsidiary   *B. subsidy*   *C. subpoena*

7. Tickets have already sold out for the first day's showing of Tom Cartmill's paintings at the National _____ .
   A. Galleon   *B. Galley*   *C. Gallery*

8. Ernest Hemingway was one of the twentieth century's most famous _____ .
   A. novels   *B. novelties*   *C. novelists*

9. The French _____ of the nineteenth century had a profound influence on the world of art.
   A. impressions   *B. impressionists*   *C. impressionisms*

10. Oldhaven Press are going to _____ my new book!
    A. publish   *B. publisher*   *C. publication*

Don't forget to keep a record of the words and expressions that you have learnt, review your notes from time to time and try to use new vocabulary items whenever possible.

For reference, see the *Easier English Dictionary for Students* (0 7475 6624 0)

The arts

C. Now look at this extract from a radio programme and fill in the gaps with one of the words or expressions from Tasks A and B. In some cases, more than one answer may be possible. You may need to change some of the word forms.

Hello, and welcome to today's edition of 'But is it Art?'

Now, I don't usually enjoy 1_____ - all those pirouettes and pas de deux's and dying swans usually send me to sleep, but last night's 2_____ of 'Sleeping Beauty' at Nureyev Hall had me on the edge of my seat. And I'm not the only one: rave 3_____ in the national press praised the excellent choreography and the incredible stage set. It's on again tonight, but you'll have to move fast if you want a ticket!

The current 4_____ of Monetto's paintings at the Wheatley 5_____ has been a disappointment. The pictures themselves are excellent, especially the great artist's 6_____ of film stars, and of course his stunning 7_____ of a vase of daffodils, but the lighting inside the room was terrible. I would have thought that, having received a government 8_____ of almost £100,000, the Wheatley Arts Council could have invested it in some good lights.

Fans of the great twentieth-century 9_____ George Orwell will be delighted to hear that Swansong Press are going to release a collection of his greatest 10_____ , which will of course include 'Animal Farm' and 'Nineteen Eighty Four'. Also included are some rare short stories which were not 11_____ until after his death. Look out for the book, which will be in the shops from the end of the month.

On the subject of books, a new 12_____ of the life of conductor Charles Worsenmost is due to be released in January. Worsenmost conducted his last 13_____ in 1998 after a long and eventful career. This is highly recommended for anyone who is remotely interested in classical music.

Have you ever wanted to be an 14_____ singer? Well, now's your chance! The National Music Company are looking for tenors and sopranos to audition for a new production of Mozart's 'Marriage of Figaro'. If you're interested, we'll give you the number to call at the end of the programme.

Potential Michelangelo's and Henry Moore's can try their hand at 15_____ this weekend. The Gleneagles Museum is holding a series of workshops which will give you the chance to chip away at a lump of stone to produce a piece of three-dimensional art. There's no need to book - just turn up at the door on Saturday at nine o'clock.

And now here's that number I promised you...

Don't forget to keep a record of the words and expressions that you have learnt, review your notes from time to time and try to use new vocabulary items whenever possible.

For reference, see the *Easier English Dictionary for Students* (0 7475 6624 0)

Town & country

A. Match the sentences in the left-hand column with the most appropriate sentence in the right-hand column. Use the words in bold to help you.

1. London is a truly *cosmopolitan* city.	A. *Drug abuse* is also a big problem.
2. A modern *metropolis* needs a good integrated transport system.	B. Shops, libraries, hospitals and entertainment complexes are just a few of them.
3. London suffers a lot from traffic *congestion*.	C. Chief among these are concerts and exhibitions.
4. *Poverty* in the *inner-city* areas can *breed crime.*	D. In particular, I enjoy the *atmosphere* that is unique to the city.
5. Cities around the world have seen a huge *population explosion.*	E. Prices in London are particularly exorbitant.
6. Birmingham has plenty of *amenities*.	F. Without them, they are unable to function properly as cities.
7. A lot of people visit Paris for its *cultural events.*	G. It is especially bad during the *rush hour,* when thousands of *commuters* try to enter or leave the city.
8. Cities in poorer countries often lack basic *infrastructures.*	H. Stress-related illnesses are very common in cities like New York.
9. The *pressures of modern city life* can be difficult to deal with.	I. Nowadays there are more *city dwellers* than ever before.
10. The *cost of living* in some places can be very high.	J. Everywhere you go there are *building sites, pedestrian precincts, blocks of flats* and *housing estates* spreading into the countryside.
11. A lot of people appreciate the *anonymity* of living in a large city.	K. They like to feel that they can do something without everybody knowing about it.
12. I love the *urban lifestyle* I lead.	L. Most people use buses and the underground to get to the banks and offices where they work.
13. In Singapore, private cars are banned from the *Central Business District* at *peak periods.*	M. Unfortunately, this is something that most large capital cities lack.
14. *Urban sprawl* is prevalent in most cities.	N. It's a *melting pot* for people from all parts of the world.

Don't forget to keep a record of the words and expressions that you have learnt, review your notes from time to time and try to use new vocabulary items whenever possible.

For reference, see the *Easier English Dictionary for Students* (0 7475 6624 0)

Town & country

B. Match the sentences in the left-hand column with an appropriate response in the right-hand column. Use the words in *bold* to help you.

1. I enjoy a *rural* lifestyle.

2. There isn't much *pollution* if you live outside a town.

3. There is a lot of *productive land* in this area.

4. In recent years, there has been a lot of *migration* from the towns to the cities.

5. The government has promised to leave the green belt alone.

6. There has been a huge reduction in the amount of *arable land* over the last twenty years.

7. My uncle's farm covers almost 800 *hectares.*

8. What are the main *crops* grown in this area?

A. Really? So why are we seeing so much *construction* in the countryside around London?

B. I'm not so sure. All those *pesticides* and *chemical fertilisers* that farmers use nowadays can't be good for the *environment.*

C. That's probably because we import more food from abroad.

D. Mostly *wheat, oats* and *barley.*

E. Really? How much is that in *acres*?

F. I'm not surprised. With such terrible *prospects* within towns, *depopulation* is inevitable.

G. Well I can't see much evidence of *cultivation.*

H. Really? I always find there's nothing to do in the countryside.

C. Now read this article and fill in the gaps with one of the words or expressions from Tasks A and B. In some cases, more than one answer may be possible. You may need to change some of the word forms.

For seven years I lived in Singapore, a 1_____ of almost three million people. Like London, Paris and New York, Singapore is a 2_____ city, with people from different parts of the world living and working together. I enjoyed the 3_____ lifestyle I led there, and made the most of the superb 4_____ , ranging from the excellent shops to some of the best restaurants in the world. In the evenings and at weekends there were always 5_____ ; with such diverse attractions as classical western music, an exhibition of Malay art or a Chinese opera in the street, it was difficult to get bored. Perhaps most impressive, however, was the remarkable transport 6_____ , with excellent roads, a swift and efficient bus service and a state-of-the-art underground system which could whisk 7_____ from the suburbs straight into the heart of the city (this was particularly important, as the government banned private cars from entering the 8_____ during the morning and afternoon 9_____ in order to reduce 10_____ on the roads and 11_____ from the exhausts).

Of course, living in a city like this has its disadvantages as well. For a start, the 12_____ can be very high - renting an apartment, for example, is very expensive. And as the city is expanding, there are a lot of 13_____ where new apartments are continually being built to deal with the 14_____ which is a direct result of the government encouraging people to have more children.

Fortunately, Singapore doesn't suffer from problems that are common in many cities such as 15_____ , which is partly the result of the government imposing very severe penalties on anyone bringing narcotics into the country, so it is safe to walk the streets at night. In fact, the 16_____ housing estates there are probably the safest and most orderly in the world.

Singapore wouldn't be ideal for everyone, however, especially if you come from the countryside and are used to a 17_____ lifestyle. The traditional villages that were once common have disappeared as the residents there realised there were no 18_____ for their future and moved into new government housing in the city. Nowadays, there is very little 19_____ around the city, which means that Singapore imports almost all of its food. And despite a 'green' approach to city planning, the 20_____ which has eaten into the countryside has had a detrimental effect on the 21_____ .

For reference, see the *Easier English Dictionary for Students* (0 7475 6624 0)

Architecture

A. Put the words in the box into their appropriate category in the table beneath. Some words can go into more than one category.

> modernist • reinforced concrete • practical • post-modern • standardised
>
> skyscraper • well-designed • porch • façade • traditional • walls
>
> an eyesore • timber • elegant • stone • steel • functional • ugly
>
> glass • concrete • low-rise   apartments • high-tech • controversial
>
> high-rise apartments   •   pleasing geometric forms   •   art deco
>
> multi-storey car park • international style • energy-efficient • foundations

---

Building materials
(6 words / expressions)

Aesthetic perception
(how we feel about a building)
(6 words / expressions)

Types of building
(4 words / expressions)

Architectural style
(6 words / expressions)

Parts of a building
(4 words / expressions)

Features (that make the building easy to live or work in)
(4 words / expressions)

For reference, see the *Easier English Dictionary for Students* (0 7475 6624 0)

Architecture

B. (Level: Intermediate / Upper-intermediate): Complete these sentences with an appropriate word or expression from A, B or C.

1. The building is _____ . It's been ruined and abandoned for years.

   A. destabilized   B. derelict   C. defunct

2. She lives on a large housing _____ near the centre of the city.

   A. estate   B. state   C. estuary

3. There are several run-down districts inside the city where the housing is in a bad state, although most of these _____ are going to be replaced by high-rise apartments.

   A. slumps   B. scrums   C. slums

4. The city council are going to _____ the old church and built a new one in its place.

   A. demobilize   B. demote   C. demolish

5. You can't knock down that house; there's a _____ order on it which makes it illegal to destroy it.

   A. preservation   B. preservative   C. presentable

6. Sir Richard Rogers is the _____ who designed the Lloyds building in London.

   A. architect   B. architecture   C. architectural

7. Some of the problems in our _____ are drug-related.

   A. inter-cities   B. internal cities   C. inner cities

8. The council hope to reduce crime in the town by introducing new _____ facilities so that people have something to do in the evening.

   A. sociable   B. socialist   C. social

9. The cinema is going to be closed for two months while the owners _____ it.

   A. renovate   B. remonstrate   C. reiterate

10. If you want to add an extension to your house, you will need _____ permission from your local council.

    A. planning   B. construction   C. plotting

Don't forget to keep a record of the words and expressions that you have learnt, review your notes from time to time and try to use new vocabulary items whenever possible.

For reference, see the *Easier English Dictionary for Students* (0 7475 6624 0)

Architecture

C. Now look at this report and fill in the gaps with one of the words or expressions from Tasks A and B. In some cases, more than one answer may be possible. You may need to change some of the word forms.

Report from the director of the West Twyford Town Planning Committee

The last year has been a busy one for the West Twyford Town Planning Committee. Outlined below are a few of the areas we have concentrated on.

1. Applications for 1_____ permission from home owners who want to develop their properties have increased by 50%. However, many of these homes are historic buildings and have 2_____ orders which prevent them from being altered externally. At present, we can only allow owners to 3_____ the inside of their homes (including installing central heating and improved wall insulation).

2. Last summer we invited several 4_____ to design plans for the new council offices on Peach Street. We eventually chose Barnard, Jackson and Willis, a local company. It was generally agreed that their design, which included a grey tinted 5_____ 6_____ at the front of the building, was the most aesthetically pleasing. They are currently in the process of laying the 7_____ for the new building, which we understand is taking some time as the land must be drained first.

3. In response to a lot of complaints about the lack of 8_____ facilities in the town, it was agreed at last month's meeting that funds should be set aside for the construction of a new sports centre and youth club.

4. Several 9_____ buildings which have been ruined and abandoned for over five years are to be knocked down. In their place, a new housing 10_____ will be built. This will provide twenty new homes within the next two years.

5. Everybody agrees that the new shops on the High Street are 11_____ . It is certainly true that they are very ugly and out of keeping with the other buildings on the street. In future, we must ensure that all new buildings are built in a 12_____ style so that they fit in with the older buildings around them.

6. There has been an increased crime rate in the 13_____ to the east of the town. We plan to demolish these run-down areas within the next eight years and re-house the residents in new 14_____ apartments in the Berkely Heath district.

7. In an attempt to help the environment, we are going to make the town hall more 15_____ . Windows will be double-glazed, walls and ceilings will be insulated and we will replace the current central heating system.

My next report will be in two months' time. Anybody wishing to discuss these issues can contact me on extension 287.

> *Don't forget to keep a record of the words and expressions that you have learnt, review your notes from time to time and try to use new vocabulary items whenever possible.*

For reference, see the *Easier English Dictionary for Students* (0 7475 6624 0)

Men & women

A. Look at the words and expressions in *bold* in the following sentences and decide if we generally consider them to have a <u>positive</u> connotation or a <u>negative</u> connotation.

1. At the interview, the manager was impressed by her *astute* comments.

2. In the *power struggle* between men and women, neither side will win.

3. After the takeover, the staff hoped that things would improve, but the new manager was just as *ruthless* as the man he replaced.

4. Some men believe that women are the *weaker sex* and should leave real work to men.

5. Our boss is a *male chauvinist* and believes that women should get less money than men for the same job.

6. John doesn't consider women to be very intelligent. To him, they are just *sex objects*.

7. Our company is *male-dominated*; all the top management positions are occupied by men.

8. Maureen is a *versatile* worker. She is able to do a number of different jobs, often at the same time.

9. He holds *egalitarian* views and believes that everybody should be treated equally.

10. The new management has taken steps to ensure *equality* in the office; from now on, everyone will receive the same money regardless of their sex or age.

11. *Militant feminists* have thrown paint at a well-known television personality in order to stress their views.

POSITIVE	NEGATIVE

Don't forget to keep a record of the words and expressions that you have learnt, review your notes from time to time and try to use new vocabulary items whenever possible.

For reference, see the *Easier English Dictionary for Students* (0 7475 6624 0)

Men & women

B. Use the words and expressions in the box to complete the conversation below.

gender roles • child-rearing • male counterparts
breadwinner • stereotypes • household management • role division
battle of the sexes • Sex Discrimination Act • social convention

Chris: Cleaning and cooking are a woman's job. After all, men are no good at 1. _____ .

Terry: What rubbish! Thank goodness the 2. _____ exists to prevent men from taking advantage of women.

Chris: Well, let's face it, in the workplace women never do as well as their 3. _____ .

Terry: And I suppose you think that women are only good for changing babies' nappies and other tedious aspects of 4. _____ .

Chris: No, but I do believe that in a modern household there should be a clearly-defined 5. _____ . Men are good at DIY, for example. Most women aren't. And I'll always believe that it's the man who should be the 6. _____ , providing food and shelter for his family.

Terry: Well, all I can say is that I'm glad your ideas of 7. _____ are not shared by most people.

Chris: Nonsense! A lot of people believe in traditional 8. _____ ; the man goes out to work, the woman stays at home. It's as simple as that.

Terry: Men at work and women at home? Come on dear, those are such typical 9. _____ ! With people like you around, the 10. _____ will always continue.

Chris: Oh, shut up dad.

Terry: Sorry Christine, but it's an issue I feel strongly about.

> *Don't forget to keep a record of the words and expressions that you have learnt, review your notes from time to time and try to use new vocabulary items whenever possible.*

For reference, see the *Easier English Dictionary for Students* (0 7475 6624 0)

Men & Women

C. Now read this essay and complete the gaps with one of the words or expressions from Tasks A and B.

'Men and women are, and always will be, different in the way they behave and are treated'.
Do you agree with this statement?

A totally (1)_____society, in which sexual (2)_____between men and women is the norm, is still a long way off. This is certainly the case if you watch television, where men are often portrayed as the (3)_____ , bringing money home to the wife, who is usually depicted as the (4)_____ , prone to extreme emotions and temper tantrums. But is this really the case? Is it still fair to create (5)_____such as this? After all, as more women go out to work and more men stay at home to look after the house and the kids, it is quite clear that so-called (6)_____are merging and disappearing.

Take the office workplace as an example. For years, businesses and companies were (7)_____ - the directors, managers and businessmen were always men, the secretaries and personal assistants always female. This was probably because men have traditionally been seen as more (8)_____ , more able to deal with the cut-and-thrust of business. But now women are proving that they can be equally tough, while simultaneously being more (9)_____ and caring. In fact, in many ways, women are more (10)_____ than men, a vital aspect of modern business where you are expected to do more than just one job. And thanks to the (11)_____ , women are paid the same as men. It would appear that, in many cases, the (12)_____is a dying breed.

At home, too, there is less evidence of (13)_____ . It is no longer the woman who does all the cooking and cleaning and (14)_____ . Such (15)_____ is now often shared equally. (16)_____ no longer requires the woman to stay indoors all day while the man stays out until all hours. Whether this is due to the struggle by the (17)_____ in the 1960s and 1970s, or whether it is due to a natural shift in attitudes is unclear.

What is clear, however, is that women no longer feel they need to be regarded as (18)_____ , the underdogs in a (19)_____with their (20)._____ . In fact, many believe that in the (21)_____ , it is women who have come out on top.

> *Don't forget to keep a record of the words and expressions that you have learnt, review your notes from time to time and try to use new vocabulary items whenever possible.*

For reference, see the *Easier English Dictionary for Students* (0 7475 6624 0)

Geography

A. Put the words in each line in the box in order according to their size (the smallest first, the largest last). In each list there is one word that does not belong with the others.

1. forest	•	tree	•	copse	•	beach	•	wood
2. road	•	peak	•	footpath	•	track	•	lane
3 mountain	•	hillock	•	shore	•	hill	•	mountain range
4. gorge	•	plain	•	waterfall	•	hollow	•	valley
5. gulf	•	ridge	•	inlet	•	bay	•	cove
6. cliff	•	brook	•	river	•	estuary	•	stream
7. city	•	continent	•	tributary	•	county	•	country
8. pond	•	puddle	•	ocean	•	sea	•	cape	•	lake

Can you think of any examples of the following in your country?

Forest	
Mountain	
Mountain range	
Valley	
Gorge	
Plain	
Gulf	
River	
Estuary	
Sea	
Lake	

B. Put the words and expressions in the box into their correct category in the tables on the next page. Some can be included in more than one category.

depopulation • mountainous • urban sprawl • fertile • ridge • cliff
densely populated • coast • under-developed • summit • industrialised
peninsula • shore • vegetation • glacier • beach • plateau
irrigation • conurbation • cape • source • coastline • tributary
waterfall • mouth • peak • overcrowding • highlands

For reference, see the *Easier English Dictionary for Students* (0 7475 6624 0)

Geography

Geographical features associated with water and the sea	Geographical features associated with land, hills and mountains

Words associated with agriculture and rural land	Words associated with towns and cities

C. Now look at this report of a journey and fill in the gaps with one of the words or expressions from Tasks A and B. In some cases, more than one answer may be possible. You may need to change some of the word forms.

We began our journey in the capital, Trinifuegos, a 1_____ conurbation of almost ten million. It is not a pretty place; heavily 2_____ , with huge factories belching out black fumes, and miles of 3_____ as housing estates and shopping centres spread out from the 4_____ centre for miles. It was a relief to leave.

As soon as we got into the countryside, things improved considerably. The climate is dry and it is difficult to grow anything, but thanks to 5_____ , which helps bring water in from the Rio Cauto (the huge river with its 6_____ high up in the snow-covered 7_____ of the Sierra Maestra 8_____), the land is fertile enough to grow the sugar cane on which much of the economy is based. We saw few people, however, as many have moved to the towns and cities to look for more profitable work. It is largely due to this rural 9_____ that the sugar-cane industry is suffering.

Further south and we entered the Holguin 10_____ , with mountains rising high above us on both sides. The land here drops sharply to the sea and the slow-moving waters of the Rio Cauto give way to 11_____ which tumble over cliffs, and small, fast-moving 12_____ which are not even wide enough to take a boat. At this point, the road we were travelling along became a 13_____ which was only just wide enough for our vehicle, and then an unpaved 14_____ which almost shook the vehicle to pieces.

And then suddenly, the Pacific 15_____ was in front of us. Our destination was the town of Santiago de Gibara, built on a 16_____ sticking out into the blue waters. The countryside here undulates gently, with low 17_____ covered in rich tropical jungle. The open 18_____ surrounding the 19_____ of the Rio Cauto as it reaches the ocean is rich and 20_____ , ideal for growing the tobacco plants which need a lot of warm, damp soil.

That night I lay in my cheap hotel, listening to the waves gently lapping the 21_____ , and when I eventually fell asleep, I dreamt of the people who had first inhabited this 22_____ almost two thousand years before.

For reference, see the *Easier English Dictionary for Students* (0 7475 6624 0)

Business & industry

A. Look at sentences 1-16, and replace the words and expressions in *bold* with a word or expression in the box which has an opposite meaning.

unskilled labourers • employees / workers / staff • credit • exports • loss demand for • bust / recession • shop floor • state-owned industries private • expenditure • lending • net • take on • retail • white-collar

1. We have a limited **supply of** computer base units. _____

2. Last year, our company made a huge **profit**. _____

3. Our **gross** profits are up by almost 150% on last year. _____

4. Banks across the country are reporting a sharp drop in **borrowing**. _____

5. The company will **debit** your bank account with £528 each month. _____

6. The **wholesale** market has experienced a downturn since the recession began. _____

7. The government is encouraging short-term investors to put their money into the **public** sector. _____

8. **Private enterprises** are under a lot of financial pressure. _____

9. **Skilled workers** are demanding a 15% pay rise. _____

10. If this continues, we will have to **lay off** members of staff. _____

11. **Blue-collar** workers across the country are demanding improved working conditions. _____

12. He works for a company which **imports** camera equipment. _____

13. A lot of people have benefited from the recent **boom** in the electrical industry. _____

14. The **management** refuse to compromise on the quality of their products. _____

15. Overall **revenue** is down by almost 15%. _____

16. A fight broke out in the **boardroom** over terms and conditions of employment. (Note: you will have to change the preposition *in* to *on*) _____

Don't forget to keep a record of the words and expressions that you have learnt, review your notes from time to time and try to use new vocabulary items whenever possible.

For reference, see the *Easier English Dictionary for Students* (0 7475 6624 0)

Business & industry

B. Match the words and expressions in the first box with a dictionary definition from the list A - Q below.

1. automation	7. interest rates	13. output
2. unemployment	8. primary industries	14. income tax
3. inflation	9. secondary industries	15. VAT
4. balance of payments	10. service industries	16. deficit
5. taxation	11. nationalised industries	17. key industries
6. GNP	12. monopoly	

A. The percentage charged for borrowing money. (*The Bank of England has raised* _____ .)

B. Industries involved in the manufacture of goods. (_____ *rely on the ready supply of raw materials.*)

C. The value of goods and services paid for in a country, including income earned in other countries. (*Last year's* _____ *was close to £25 billion.*)

D. The amount which a firm, machine or person produces. (*The factory has doubled its* _____ *in the last six months.*)

E. Industries involved in the production of raw materials. (*Coal mining is an important* _____ .)

F Installing machinery in place of workers (_____ *can be a mixed blessing - machines usually tend to be out of order when you need them most.*)

G. Industries which do not make products but offer a service such as banking, insurance and transport. (_____ *have become more important in the last decade.*)

H. The difference in value between a country's imports and exports. (*The government is trying to reduce the* _____ *deficit.*)

I. The amount by which expenditure is more than receipts in a firm's or country's accounts. (*The company announced a two million pound* _____ .)

J. A system where one person or company supplies all of a product in one area without any competition. (*The state has a* _____ *of the tobacco trade.*)

K. Industries which were once privately owned, but now belong to the state. (*Workers in* _____ *are to get a 3% pay rise.*)

L. Lack of work. (*The figures for* _____ *are rising.*)

M. The action of imposing taxes. (*Money raised by* _____ *pays for all government services.*)

N. The most important industries in a country. (*Oil is a* _____ *which is essential to the country's economy.*)

O. A state in an economy where prices and wages are rising to keep pace with each other. (*The government is trying to keep* _____ *down below 3%.*)

P. A tax on money earned as wages or salary. (*She pays* _____ *at the lowest rate.*)

Q. A tax imposed as a percentage of the invoice value of goods or services. An indirect tax. (_____ *in Britain currently runs at 17.5%.*)

For reference, see the *Easier English Dictionary for Students* (0 7475 6624 0)

Business & industry

C. Now look at this extract from a business programme and fill in the gaps with one of the words or expressions from Tasks A and B. In some cases, more than one answer may be possible. You may need to change some of the word forms.

1_____ rates are to rise by a further half a percent next month, putting further pressure on homeowners paying mortgages. It will also discourage people from 2_____ money from the high street banks, who are already under a lot of pressure. Last year, the National Bank was forced to 3_____ 2,000 members of staff across the country, adding to the country's rapidly rising rate of 4_____ .

5_____ rose in the last year by almost 6%, despite the government's pledge to keep price and wage rises no higher than 3%. This has had a negative impact on 6_____ , since the strong pound coupled with rising prices has made it almost impossible for foreign companies to buy British goods and services. Especially affected are the 7_____ producing pharmaceuticals and chemicals.

8_____ workers in 9_____ industries across the country are demanding higher 10_____ . Unions and workers are negotiating with 11_____ chiefs for an eight percent rise. This follows the announcement that the government want more investors to put their money into the 12_____ sector.

13_____ for home computers has finally overtaken the 14_____ , making it once again a seller's market. There is now a two-week waiting list to receive a new computer. This has pushed prices up by almost a third.

Bradford Aerospace Technologies, where overall 15_____ for sales of aircraft parts has dropped by almost 10% in the last quarter, will shortly become a 16_____ industry in a final desperate attempt to keep it open. The government has promised it will keep on the current workforce.

Bad news too for Ranger Cars, who this week announced a 17_____ of almost five million pounds. A spokesman for the company blamed high labour costs and the reluctance by union leaders to approve increased 18_____ at the firm's factories. They insist that the installation of new machinery will lead to redundancies.

> *Don't forget to keep a record of the words and expressions that you have learnt, review your notes from time to time and try to use new vocabulary items whenever possible.*

For reference, see the *Easier English Dictionary for Students* (0 7475 6624 0)

Global problems

A. Complete sentences 1-15 with the correct word or expression from A, B or C. In each case two of the options are incorrectly spelt.

1. Thousands of buildings were flattened in the San Francisco _____ of 1906.
   A. *earthquack*   B. *earthquake*   C. *earthquaik*

2. The _____ damaged properties all along the coast.
   A. *hurricane*   B. *hurriccane*   C. *huriccane*

3. A _____ struck the southern coast with tremendous force.
   A. *tornadoe*   B. *tornado*   C. *tornaddo*

4. The _____ caused immense damage in the regions along the coast.
   A. *taifun*   B. *typhone*   C. *typhoon*

5. The _____ has been dormant for years, but last month it showed signs of new life.
   A. *volcano*   B. *vulcano*   C. *volcanoe*

6. Several _____ were heard during the night as the army occupied the city.
   A. *explossions*   B. *explosiones*   C. *explosions*

7. The American _____ of 1861-1865 was fought between the south and the north.
   A. *civil war*   B. *sivil war*   C. *civvil war*

8. There has been a major _____ on the motorway.
   A. *acident*   B. *accident*   C. *acciddent*

9. _____ rain has brought serious problems.
   A. *Torrential*   B. *Torential*   C. *Torrantial*

10. The storm caused widespread _____ along the coast.
    A. *devvastation*   B. *devustation*   C. *devastation*

11. The _____ were caused by heavy rain.
    A. *floodes*   B. *floods*   C. *flouds*

12. Relief workers are bringing food to _____-stricken areas.
    A. *draught*   B. *drought*   C. *drouhgt*

13. _____ is widespread in parts of Africa, with millions suffering from malnutrition.
    A. *famine*   B. *fammine*   C. *faminne*

14. The authorities are taking steps to prevent an _____ of cholera.
    A. *epidemmic*   B. *epidemic*   C. *eppidemic*

15. The _____ was spread from rats to fleas and then on to humans.
    A. *plague*   B. *plaque*   C. *plaigue*

B. Complete sentences 1-10 with an appropriate word or expression from the box. In some cases, more than one answer is possible. There are five words which do not fit into any of the sentences.

| disaster • survivors • spouted • suffering • ran • erupted • broke out |
| shook • casualties • spread • refugees • relief • flamed • wobbled • swept |

1. The disease _____ rapidly, killing everybody in its path.

2. The fire _____ through the slums, destroying everything.

For reference, see the *Easier English Dictionary for Students* (0 7475 6624 0)

Global problems

3. When the volcano _____ , people panicked and tried to escape.

4. The ground _____ violently when the earthquake began.

5. Fierce fighting _____ between government soldiers and rebel forces.

6. A funeral was held for the _____ of the fire.

7. An aid convoy was sent to help _____ of the hurricane.

8. _____ from the conflict in Mantagua have been fleeing across the border.

9. The poor people in the city have experienced terrible _____ as a result of the disaster.

10. International aid agencies are trying to bring _____ to the starving population.

C. Now look at this report and fill in the gaps with one of the words or expressions from Tasks A and B. In some cases, more than one answer may be possible. You may need to change some of the word forms.

REPORT FROM THE INTERNATIONAL CHARITIES SUPPORT FOUNDATION (ICSF)

The last year has been a particularly busy one for the ICSF. Outlined below are a few of the areas we have been busy in.

1. Following 1_____ rain in eastern Mozamlumbi in January, millions were made homeless as 2_____ waters rose. The water also became polluted and there was a cholera 3_____ as people continued to use it for drinking and cooking. Furthermore, as the harvest had been destroyed and there was not enough food to go round, 4_____ became a problem. Charities around the world worked particularly hard to bring 5_____ to the area.

2. Mount Etsuvius, the 6_____ which had been dormant since 1968, 7_____ suddenly in April. Thousands had to be evacuated to camps thirty miles from the disaster area. They still have not been rehoused.

3. The 8_____ in the Caribbean in July, which saw wind speeds of up to 180 miles per hour, caused immense 9_____ on many islands. Islands off the Japanese coast also suffered their worst 10_____ in almost thirty years, with prolonged winds in excess of 150 miles per hour. There were many 11_____ who had to be evacuated to hospitals which were not properly equipped to deal with the disasters.

4. The 12_____ in the northern part of Somopia continued into its second year, with millions of acres of crops destroyed by lack of rain. Meanwhile, the 13_____ between those loyal to the president and those supporting the rebel leader continued into its fifth year. 14_____ from the conflict have been fleeing across the border, with stories of atrocities committed by both sides.

5. In October, a fire 15_____ through Londum, the ancient capital of Perania. The 16_____ , which probably started in a bakery, destroyed thousands of homes. There were several 17_____ when the fire reached a fireworks factory, and a number of people were killed.

6. An outbreak of bubonic 18_____ was reported in the eastern provinces of Indocuba in November. It is believed to have been caused by a sudden increase in the number of rats breeding in the sewers.

A full report will be available in February, and will be presented to the appropriate departments of the United Nations shortly afterwards.

101

For reference, see the *Easier English Dictionary for Students* (0 7475 6624 0)

Answers

Page 1 Condition answers

A.

1. You can borrow my dictionary **providing that** you return it before you go home. (We can also say *provided that*)
2. You can't go to university **unless** you have good grades. (*Unless* means the same as *If you don't*)
3. Pollution will get worse **as long as** we continue to live in a throwaway society. (We can also say *so long as*, although this is slightly more formal)
4. Many developed countries are willing to waive the Third World debt **on condition that** the money is reinvested in education and medicine.
5. Some countries will never be able to rectify their deficits, **no matter how** hard they work. (Note word changes and sentence ending)
6. Computers are difficult things to understand, **however many** books you read about them. (*However* is used in the same way as *no matter*)
7. Crime is a problem, **wherever** you go.

On condition that is the most formal expression, and is generally stronger than the other words and expressions.

B. (We put the conditional clause at the beginning of a sentence if we consider it to be the most important part of the sentence)

1. **Providing that** you return it before you go home, you can borrow my dictionary.
2. **Unless** you have good grades, you can't go to university.
3. **As long as** we continue to live in a throwaway society, pollution will get worse.
4. **On condition that** the money is reinvested in education and medicine, many developed countries are willing to waive the Third World debt.
5. **No matter how** hard they work, some countries will never be able to rectify their deficits.
6. **However many** books you read about them, computers are difficult things to understand.
7. **Wherever** you go, crime is a problem.

C. From your own ideas.

D. 1. prerequisites   2. conditions   3. requirement

Page 2 Changes answers

1. adapt   2. adjust   3. transform   4. switch   5. alter   6. vary   7. exchange   8. expand   9. increase   10. dissolve
11. swell   12. disappear   13. renew   14. renovate   15. promote (in the second sentence, *promote* means to make sure people know about something by advertising it)   16. demote   17. fade   18. replace   19. cure (in the second sentence, *cure* means to preserve meat or fish by putting it in salt)   20. reduce

Other words and expressions which you might find useful include:
swap / shrink / melt / grow / heal / decline / enlarge / downsize / take to something

Page 4 Describing & analysing tables answers

A. 1. Cilicia + Cappadocia   2. Cappadocia   3. Lycia   4. Moesia   5. Cappadocia   6. Moesia   7. Lycia   8. Moesia   9. Lycia + Moesia   10. Lycia   11. Lycia   12. Cilicia   13. Cappadocia

> The verbs *rise* and *increase* have the same meaning here. We can also say *climb*. These verbs can also be nouns.
>
> The verbs *fall, drop* and *decline* have the same meaning here. These verbs can also be nouns.
>
> The adverbs *steadily* and *noticeably* can have the same meaning here. They can also be adjectives (*steady, noticeable*).
>
> The adverbs *sharply, rapidly* and *dramatically* can have the same meaning here. They can also be adjectives (*sharp, rapid, dramatic*).

For reference, see the *Easier English Dictionary for Students* (0 7475 6624 0)

Vocabulary record sheet

Photocopy this sheet as many times as you like, and use it to keep a record of new words and expressions that you learn. Try to build your own vocabulary bank of useful words and expressions. Keep this in a file in alphabetical order for quick reference. Review the words and expressions that you have recorded on a regular basis.

Language area *(eg, Work, Education, Idioms, Phrasal verbs, etc):*	

1. Word or expression	
2. Definition	
3. Equivalent in my language	
4. Sample sentence	

1. Word or expression	
2. Definition	
3. Equivalent in my language	
4. Sample sentence	

1. Word or expression	
2. Definition	
3. Equivalent in my language	
4. Sample sentence	

1. Word or expression	
2. Definition	
3. Equivalent in my language	
4. Sample sentence	

You may photcopy this page